YORK NOTES

D0237556

AN INSPECTOR CALLS

J. B. PRIESTLEY

WORKBOOK BY MARY GREEN

PEARSON

YORK
PRESS

The right of Mary Green to be identified as the Author of this Work has been asserted by her in accordance with the Copyright, Designs and Patents Act 1988

YORK PRESS
322 Old Brompton Road, London SW5 9JH

PEARSON EDUCATION LIMITED
Edinburgh Gate, Harlow,
Essex CM20 2JE, United Kingdom
Associated companies, branches and representatives throughout the world

© Librairie du Liban *Publishers* 2014, 2015

Quotations from *An Inspector Calls* by J. B. Priestley (© J. B. Priestley, 1965) are reprinted by permission of United Agents on behalf of: The Estate of the Late J. B. Priestley

All rights reserved. No part of this publication may be reproduced, stored in a retrieval system, or transmitted in any form or by any means, electronic, mechanical, photocopying, recording, or otherwise, without either the prior written permission of the Publishers or a licence permitting restricted copying in the United Kingdom issued by the Copyright Licensing Agency Ltd, Saffron House, 6–10 Kirby Street, London EC1N 8TS

First published 2014
This new and fully revised edition 2015
Reprinted 2016

10 9 8 7

ISBN 978–1–2921–0079–1

Illustrations by Timo Grubing; and Rob Foote (page 54 only)

Typeset by Carnegie Book Production
Printed in Slovakia by Neografia.

Photo credits: StudioSmart/Shutterstock for page 8 / © INTERFOTO/Alamy for page 11 / Dynamicfoto/Shutterstock for page 21 / Neveshkin Nikolay/Shutterstock for page 23 / Super3D/Shutterstock for page 27 / Gemenacom/Shutterstock for page 31 / Markus Pfaff/Shutterstock for page 37 / Sasha/Hulton Archive/Getty images for page 49 / Gouraud Studio/Shutterstock for page 51 / anderm/Shutterstock for page 55 / Anneka/Shutterstock for page 60

CONTENTS

Preparing for assessment

HOW WILL I BE ASSESSED ON MY WORK ON *AN INSPECTOR CALLS*?

All exam boards are different, but whichever course you are following, your work will be examined through these four Assessment Objectives:

Assessment Objectives	Wording	Worth thinking about ...
AO1	Read, understand and respond to texts. Students should be able to: ● maintain a critical style and develop an informed personal response ● use textual references, including quotations, to support and illustrate interpretations.	● How well do I know what happens, what people say, do, etc.? ● What do *I* think about the key ideas in the play? ● How can I support my viewpoint in a really convincing way? ● What are the best quotations to use and when should I use them?
AO2	Analyse the language, form and structure used by a writer to create meanings and effects, using relevant subject terminology where appropriate.	● What specific things does the writer 'do'? What choices has Priestley made? (Why this particular word, phrase or paragraph here? Why does this event happen at this point?) ● What effects do these choices create? Suspense? Nervous laughter? Reflective mood?
AO3	Show understanding of the relationships between texts and the contexts in which they were written.	● What can I learn about society from the play? (What does it tell me about workers' rights in the 1910s, for example?) ● What was society like in Priestley's time? Can I see it reflected in the play?
AO4	Use a range of vocabulary and sentence structures for clarity, purpose and effect, with accurate spelling and punctuation.	● How accurately and clearly do I write? ● Are there small errors of grammar, spelling and punctuation I can get rid of?

Look out for the Assessment Objective labels throughout your York Notes Workbook – these will help to focus your study and revision!

The text used in this Workbook is the Heinemann edition, 1992.

How to use your York Notes Workbook

There are lots of ways your Workbook can support your study and revision of *An Inspector Calls*. There is no 'right' way – choose the one that suits your learning style best.

1) Alongside the York Notes Study Guide and the text	2) As a 'stand-alone' revision programme	3) As a form of mock-exam
Do you have the York Notes Study Guide for *An Inspector Calls*? The contents of your Workbook are designed to match the sections in the Study Guide, so with the play to hand you could: • read the relevant section(s) of the Study Guide and any part of the play referred to • complete the tasks in the same section in your Workbook.	Think you know *An Inspector Calls* well? Why not work through the Workbook systematically, either as you finish scenes, or as you study or revise certain aspects in class or at home? You could make a revision diary and allocate particular sections of the Workbook to a day or week.	Prefer to do all your revision in one go? You could put aside a day or two and work through the Workbook, page by page. Once you have finished, check all your answers in one go! This will be quite a challenge, but it may be the approach you prefer.

HOW WILL THE WORKBOOK HELP YOU TEST AND CHECK YOUR KNOWLEDGE AND SKILLS?

Parts Two to **Five** offer a range of tasks and activities:

These fun and quick-to-complete tasks check your basic knowledge of the text

These more open questions challenge you to show your understanding

This task focuses on a key character, theme, technique, idea or relationship and helps you plan and write up paragraphs from an essay

A clear, quick way to record your progress visually

Each Part ends with a **Practice task** to extend your revision:

An exam-style task is provided at the end of each section for you to practise a full essay

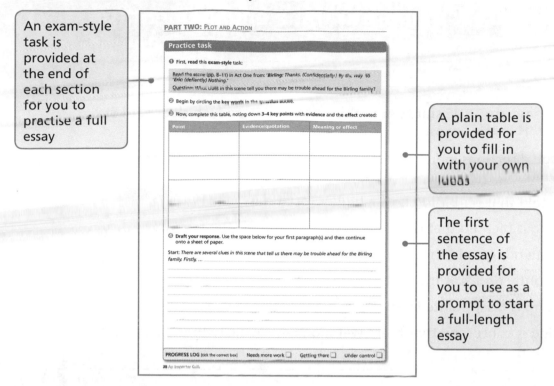

A plain table is provided for you to fill in with your own ideas

The first sentence of the essay is provided for you to use as a prompt to start a full-length essay

Part Six: Progress Booster helps you test your own key writing skills:

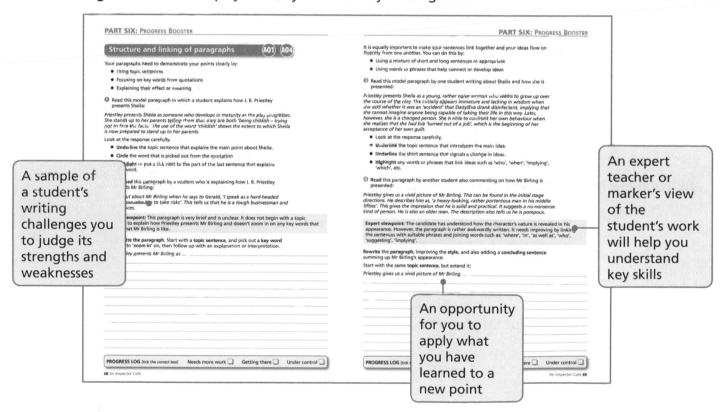

A sample of a student's writing challenges you to judge its strengths and weaknesses

An expert teacher or marker's view of the student's work will help you understand key skills

An opportunity for you to apply what you have learned to a new point

Don't forget – these are just some examples of the Workbook contents. Inside there is much more to help you revise. For example:

● lots of examples of students' own work at different levels

● help with spelling, punctuation and grammar

● advice and tasks on writing about context

● a full answer key so you can check your answers

● a full-length practice exam task with guidance on what to focus on.

Act One, Part 1: Celebrating the engagement (pp. 1–7)

QUICK TEST ✓

1 Which of these are **TRUE** statements about this scene, and which are **FALSE**? Write 'T' or 'F' in the boxes:

a) The stage directions indicate that the Birling family are warm hearted and loving. ☐

b) We are told that Mr Birling is of a higher social class than his wife. ☐

c) Mr Birling is pleased that Gerald is to become part of the family. ☐

d) Sheila reminds Gerald that he neglected her last summer. ☐

e) Eric is slightly drunk at the dinner party. ☐

f) Mrs Birling is disappointed with Sheila's engagement ring. ☐

g) Mr Birling is concerned that there will soon be trouble with the workforce. ☐

THINKING MORE DEEPLY ❓

2 Write **one** or **two sentences** in response to each of these questions:

a) What do you learn about the social position of the Birling family?

....

....

....

....

b) What impression do we get of Sheila and Gerald's relationship?

....

....

....

....

c) What do we learn about Eric from his behaviour at the dinner party?

....

....

....

....

....

....

EXAM PREPARATION: WRITING ABOUT ATTITUDES

Reread Mr Birling's monologues (speeches) (pp. 6–7) from *'There's a good deal of silly talk'* to *'which will always be behindhand naturally.'*

Question: How do Mr Birling's comments help you to understand attitudes among many of the wealthy before the First World War?

Think about:

● How he regards himself and those in his position

● What he thinks the future will hold

Complete this table:

Point/detail	Evidence	Effect or explanation
1: *Mr Birling believes the powerful and wealthy should protect their position.*	*'We employers at last are coming together to see that our interests ... are properly protected.'*	*His comments imply that he disregards the workforce he employs.*
2: *He likes to speak at length and expects to be listened to.*		
3: *He is confident that future technology will bring prosperity.*		

Write up **point 1** into a **paragraph** below, in your own words. Remember to include what you infer from the evidence, or the writer's effects.

....

....

....

....

....

Now, choose **one** of your **other points** and write it out as another **paragraph** here:

....

....

....

....

....

....

PROGRESS LOG [tick the correct box]   Needs more work ☐   Getting there ☐   Under control ☐

Act One, Part 2: A confidential chat (pp. 8–11)

QUICK TEST ✓

❶ Choose the correct answer to **finish the statement** and tick the box:

a) Mr Birling held the position of: Chief Constable ☐   Lord Mayor ☐
Member of Parliament ☐

b) Mr Birling expects to receive a: knighthood ☐   royal visit ☐
visit from Lady Croft ☐

c) Gerald and Mr Birling joke about a: possible death ☐   possible scandal ☐
visit from the Inspector ☐

d) Mrs Birling and Sheila are discussing: Lady Croft ☐   clothes ☐   Eric ☐

e) Eric arouses curiosity when he: refuses to join the men for port ☐
claims not to remember something ☐   leaves by the back door ☐

THINKING MORE DEEPLY ?

❷ Write **one** or **two sentences** in response to each of these questions:

a) How do we know that Mr Birling feels inferior to Gerald's family?

....

....

....

....

....

b) How does Gerald behave with Mr Birling in this scene?

....

....

....

....

....

c) How can we tell there is something wrong with Eric before the
Inspector arrives?

....

....

....

....

EXAM PREPARATION: WRITING ABOUT MR BIRLING'S ATTITUDES · A01

Reread Mr Birling's speech (p. 8) from *'I was Lord Mayor here'* to *'chance of a knighthood'* and his speech (pp. 9–10) from *'I don't want to lecture'* to *'and look after himself and his own'*.

Question: What do Mr Birling's comments reveal about his character?

Think about:

- What he says about himself and what he expects
- What he says about the community

❸ Complete this table:

Point/detail	Evidence	Effect or explanation
1: *He believes he will be knighted (for contributions to the community).*	*'I've always been regarded as a sound useful party man.'*	*His comments suggest that a knighthood will depend on his support for the right people and political party.*
2: *He believes in self-reliance.*		
3: *He has no respect for the community.*		

❹ Write up **point 1** into a **paragraph** below, in your own words. Remember to include what you infer from the evidence, or the writer's effects.

....
....
....
....
....

❺ Now, choose **one** of your **other points** and write it out as another **paragraph** here:

....
....
....
....
....
....
....

PROGRESS LOG [tick the correct box]   Needs more work ☐   Getting there ☐   Under control ☐

Act One, Part 3: An inspector interrupts (pp. 11–16)

QUICK TEST ✓

❶ Complete this **gap-fill** paragraph about the scene, adding the **correct or suitable information**:

We first meet Inspector .... when Edna, the maid, announces him. Although not a .... man, he is an imposing figure. Mr Birling tries to impress the Inspector by pointing out that he was an alderman and also Lord Mayor and still sits on the .... , meaning he is a magistrate. The Inspector explains that a girl died in the Infirmary after swallowing strong .... A letter and a diary were found in her room. She had more than one name, but her original name was .... and she worked at Mr Birling's .... The Inspector shows Mr Birling a .... of the girl. Eventually Mr Birling remembers that he sacked her because of her part in a .... for higher wages.

THINKING MORE DEEPLY ❓

❷ Write **one** or **two sentences** in response to each of these questions:

a) Why do you think Mr Birling wanted to impress the Inspector?

....

....

....

....

b) What does Gerald think about Eva Smith's sacking?

....

....

....

....

c) What does the Inspector mean by 'a chain of events' (p. 14)?

....

....

....

....

....

EXAM PREPARATION: WRITING ABOUT DIFFERENT POINTS OF VIEW A01

Reread the dialogue (p. 15) from *'Inspector: It's my duty to ask questions'* to *'Inspector: ... to ask for the earth than to take it.'*

Question: What different points of view do Mr Birling and Eric hold about Eva Smith's sacking?

Think about:

● What each character says

● What each character cares about

❸ Complete this table:

Point/detail	Evidence	Effect or explanation
1: *Mr Birling cares about the profit his company makes.*	*'it's my duty to keep labour costs down'.*	*His comments tell us that he values the profit he makes more than a good wage for his workers.*
2: *Eric is sympathetic to the hardship Eva Smith faced.*		
3: *We can further compare Mr Birling and Eric's points of view about taking responsibility for the workers.*		

❹ Write up **point 1** into a **paragraph** below, in your own words. Remember to include what you infer from the evidence, or the writer's effects.

....

....

....

....

❺ Now, choose **one** of your **other** points and write it out as another **paragraph** here:

....

....

....

....

....

PROGRESS LOG [tick the correct box]　　Needs more work ☐　　Getting there ☐　　Under control ☐

Act One, Part 4: Sheila's link in the chain (pp. 16–21)

QUICK TEST ✓

❶ Who is each character talking **about**? Write a **name** (or names) from the list below next to each quotation:

Sheila   Eva Smith   the Inspector   Eric   Gerald   factory workers

a) 'Birling: ... I've half a mind to report <u>you</u>. I've told you all I know –' (p. 17)

b) 'Sheila: (*rather distressed*) Sorry! It's just that I can't help thinking about <u>this girl</u> –' (p. 17)

c) 'Gerald: ... It's what happened to <u>her</u> since she left Mr Birling's works that is important.' (p. 18)

d) 'Birling: And are you suggesting now that one of <u>them</u> knows something about <u>this girl</u>?' (p. 18)

e) 'Sheila: But <u>these girls</u> aren't cheap labour – they're *people*.' (p. 19)

f) 'Eric: <u>She</u> recognized <u>her</u> from the photograph, didn't she?' (p. 21)

g) 'Birling: (*angrily*) Why the devil do <u>you</u> want to go upsetting <u>the child</u> like that?' (p. 21)

THINKING MORE DEEPLY ?

❷ Write **one** or **two sentences** in response to each of these questions:

a) In what way does the Inspector drive home the awfulness of Eva Smith's death?

b) How does Mr Birling's mood change when he realises that all the family might be involved with Eva Smith?

c) Why does the Inspector show the photograph to one character at a time?

EXAM PREPARATION: WRITING ABOUT SHEILA'S INVOLVEMENT

Reread (pp. 19–21) from *'Inspector: Where I was before, Mr Croft'* to the stage directions *'The other three stare in amazement for a moment.'*

Question: In what way is Sheila involved with Eva Smith and how does she react to the knowledge?

Think about:

- What Sheila says and feels

 Complete this table:

Point/detail	Evidence	Effect or explanation
1: *Sheila scolds her father for sacking Eva Smith.*	*'I think it was a mean thing to do. Perhaps that spoilt everything for her.'*	*She not only feels sympathy for Eva Smith but also recognises the possible consequences of her father's actions.*
2: *Sheila begins to realise that Eva is the girl she had sacked from Milwards.*		
3: *Sheila recognises the girl in the photograph the Inspector shows her.*		

4️⃣ Write up **point 1** into a **paragraph** below, in your own words. Remember to include what you infer from the evidence, or the writer's effects.

....

....

....

....

....

....

5️⃣ Now, choose **one** of your **other points** and write it out as another **paragraph** here:

....

....

....

....

....

....

....

PROGRESS LOG [tick the correct box]   Needs more work ☐   Getting there ☐   Under control ☐

Act One, Part 5: Sheila's confession (pp. 21–6)

QUICK TEST ✓

❶ Which of these are **TRUE** statements about this scene, and which are **FALSE**?
Write 'T' or 'F' in the boxes:

a) Mr Birling exits to tell his wife what is happening. ☐

b) Gerald doesn't want to look at the photograph and refuses to do so. ☐

c) The Inspector suggests that Eric had better stay in the room. ☐

d) Sheila refuses to accept that she is partly to blame for Eva Smith's downfall. ☐

e) Sheila insists that Eva Smith made unpleasant comments in Milwards. ☐

f) The Inspector is trying to understand why Eva Smith died. ☐

g) Sheila immediately recognises that Gerald knew Daisy Renton. ☐

THINKING MORE DEEPLY ?

❷ Write **one** or **two sentences** in response to each of these questions:

a) Why did Sheila have Eva Smith dismissed?

....

....

....

....

....

....

b) How can we tell in this scene that Sheila regrets what happened at Milwards?

....

....

....

....

....

c) What is dramatic about the ending to Act One?

....

....

....

....

....

....

EXAM PREPARATION: WRITING ABOUT THE INSPECTOR'S POWER

Reread (pp. 21–3) from the stage directions *'BIRLING looks as if about to make some retort'* to *'**Inspector:** ... Just as your father is.'*

Question: How is the Inspector gaining control and power over the situation?

Think about:

- What the character says and the tone he uses
- How he manages the other characters

③ Complete this table:

Point/detail	Evidence	Effect or explanation
1: *The Inspector deliberately refuses Gerald's request.*	*'Gerald: I'd like to have a look at that photograph now, Inspector.* *'Inspector: All in good time.'*	*The Inspector's tone is calm and he is increasingly in control of the situation.*
2: *He states his opinion regardless of whom he is speaking to.*		
3: *He states the consequences of Eva Smith's dismissal from Milwards.*		

④ Write up **point 1** into a **paragraph** below, in your own words. Remember to include what you infer from the evidence, or the writer's effects.

....

....

....

....

....

....

⑤ Now, choose **one** of your **other points** and write it out as **another paragraph** here:

....

....

....

....

....

PROGRESS LOG [tick the correct box]   Needs more work ☐   Getting there ☐   Under control ☐

Act Two, Part 1: Guilty feelings (pp. 27–9)

QUICK TEST

❶ Choose the correct answer to **finish the statement** and tick the box:

a) Act Two opens:　in the garden ☐　in the hall ☐　where Act One finished ☐

b) At the beginning of Act Two the Inspector is:　in the doorway ☐
sitting down ☐　leaving the stage ☐

c) Initially, Sheila:　frowns ☐　laughs hysterically ☐　wipes her tears ☐

d) Sheila and Gerald:　quarrel ☐　do not speak to each other ☐
leave the room together ☐

e) The Inspector:　interrupts Gerald and Sheila ☐　arrests Gerald ☐　goes out ☐

f) Mrs Birling enters:　with the maid ☐　unaware of the situation ☐　with Eric ☐

g) At first, Mrs Birling approaches the Inspector:　politely ☐　rudely ☐　fearfully ☐

h) Mrs Birling:　does not understand Sheila ☐　thinks Sheila is ill ☐
sees Sheila crying ☐

THINKING MORE DEEPLY

❷ Write **one** or **two sentences** in response to each of these questions:

a) What is Gerald afraid of?

....
....
....
....

b) What does Mrs Birling attempt to do when she enters?

....
....
....
....

c) How does Sheila react to her mother, and what is she afraid of?

....
....
....
....

EXAM PREPARATION: WRITING ABOUT SHEILA'S CHANGING ATTITUDES

Reread (pp. 27–9) from **'Inspector:** *Well, I don't want to keep you here'* to **'Sheila:** *... I don't understand about you.'*

Question: In this scene, how does Sheila come to regard her own part in Eva Smith's death?

Think about:

- What she says and how she feels
- What she needs to discover about herself and the other characters

③ Complete this table.

Point/detail	Evidence	Effect or explanation
1: *Sheila suspects that Gerald is also implicated in Eva Smith/ Daisy Renton's death.*	*She says to the Inspector: 'you haven't finished asking questions – have you? ...Then I'm staying.'*	*She wants to hear the truth, even if it is unpleasant.*
2: *But she still feels she is to blame.*		
3: *Sheila responds to the Inspector's discussion of shared responsibility.*		

④ Write up **point 1** into a **paragraph** below, in your own words. Remember to include what you infer from the evidence, or the writer's effects.

....

....

....

....

....

⑤ Now, choose **one** of your **other points** and write it out as **another paragraph** here:

....

....

....

....

....

....

....

PROGRESS LOG [tick the correct box]   Needs more work ☐   Getting there ☐   Under control ☐

Act Two, Part 2: Enter Mrs Birling (pp. 29–32)

QUICK TEST ✓

❶ Complete this **gap-fill** paragraph about the scene, with the **correct or suitable information**:

Mrs Birling enters in a .... manner, which is very different from

the mood of the others in the room. When Mrs Birling comments that the Inspector

has made an impression on her ...., he replies that this often

happens with the young. Sheila is determined to stay, despite her mother's

comment that Sheila has a morbid curiosity about the girl's ....

As the scene develops, Mrs Birling's self-importance increases and she accuses

the Inspector of being .... She reminds him that ....

was once Lord Mayor. However, she is shocked to learn of the seriousness of

.... drinking habit.

THINKING MORE DEEPLY ❓

❷ Write **one** or **two sentences** in response to each of these questions:

a) In what way does the word 'offence' have a double meaning?

....

....

....

....

....

b) Why does the Inspector question Mrs Birling about Eric's drinking?

....

....

....

....

....

c) How does Gerald respond to Mrs Birling's question about Eric's drinking?

....

....

....

....

EXAM PREPARATION: WRITING ABOUT SHEILA'S FOREWARNING

Reread the dialogue (pp. 30–1) from *'Sheila: (urgently cutting in) Mother, don't – please don't.'* to *'Mrs Birling: … Inspector will take offence – '.*

Question: Why does Sheila use the image of a 'wall' to address her mother and how does her mother respond?

Think about:

- How Sheila uses the image
- How her mother responds

❶ Complete this table:

Point/detail	Evidence	Effect or explanation
1: *Sheila is aware that Mrs Birling does not accept that the family may have played a part in Eva Smith's death.*	*'You mustn't try to build up a kind of wall between us and that girl.'*	*The 'wall' is a metaphor referring to the way in which Mrs Birling separates herself (and her family and Gerald) from possible guilt.*
2: *Sheila is warning her mother what will happen if she fails to answer the Inspector's questions.*		
3: *Mrs Birling fails to understand.*		

❹ Write up **point 1** into a **paragraph** below, in your own words. Remember to include what you infer from the evidence, or the writer's effects.

....

....

....

....

....

❺ Now, choose **one** of your **other points** and write it out as another **paragraph** here:

....

....

....

....

....

PROGRESS LOG [tick the correct box]   Needs more work ☐   Getting there ☐   Under control ☐

Act Two, Part 3: Gerald's revelations (pp. 32–40)

QUICK TEST ✓

❶ From the list of names, identify which **character** is being **referred to**. Sometimes it might be more than one person.

Sheila   **Gerald**   **Daisy Renton/Eva Smith**   **Eric**   **Alderman Meggarty**

a) 'Birling: I've been trying to persuade .... to go to bed, but he won't.' (p. 32)

b) 'Birling: What's the matter with <u>that child</u>?' (p. 33)

c) 'Inspector: … Mr Croft, when did you first get to know <u>her</u>?' (p. 33)

d) 'Sheila: Well, we didn't think <u>you</u> meant Buckingham Palace.' (p. 34)

e) 'Gerald: <u>He's</u> a notorious womanizer [and] one of the worst sots and rogues in Brumley –' (p. 35)

f) 'Inspector: Yes. <u>She</u> was a woman. She was lonely. Were <u>you</u> in love with her?' (p. 37)

g) 'Sheila: … <u>You</u> were the wonderful Fairy Prince.' (p. 38)

THINKING MORE DEEPLY ?

❷ Write **one** or **two sentences** in response to each of these questions:

a) How does Gerald's confession affect the audience?

b) How does Sheila help create the idea that the Inspector is all-knowing?

c) How does Sheila react to Gerald at the end of the scene?

EXAM PREPARATION: WRITING ABOUT THE INSPECTOR'S KNOWLEDGE **A02**

Reread the dialogue (p. 39) from *'**Gerald:** Yes, we'd agreed about that.'* to *'**Inspector:** Go where? Home?'*

Question: How does the Inspector appear to know so much about people and events? How is Gerald affected by the Inspector's knowledge?

Think about:

- The Inspector's methods, e.g. use of the diary
- How Gerald responds

❶ Complete this table:

Point/detail	Evidence	Effect or explanation
1: *The Inspector asks simple questions.*	*He asks questions of Gerald such as: 'When did this affair end?'; 'How did she take it?'; 'She had to move out of those rooms?'*	*These questions, which often build on what the characters say, encourage the characters to reveal further events and actions.*
2: *Gerald is curious about the Inspector's knowledge.*		
3: *Gerald reacts to the information about Daisy Renton.*		

❹ Write up **point 1** into a **paragraph** below, in your own words. Remember to include what you infer from the evidence, or the writer's effects.

....
....
....
....
....

❺ Now, choose **one** of your **other points** and write it out as another **paragraph** here:

....
....
....
....
....

PROGRESS LOG [tick the correct box]   Needs more work ☐   Getting there ☐   Under control ☐

Act Two, Part 4: Sheila opposes her mother (pp. 40–2)

QUICK TEST ✓

❶ Which of these are **TRUE** statements about this scene, and which are **FALSE**?
Write **'T'** or **'F'** in the boxes:

a) Mr Birling tries to defend Eric to Sheila. ☐

b) Sheila points out that the Inspector did not show Gerald the photograph. ☐

c) Mrs Birling does not wish to look at the photograph. ☐

d) Sheila defends her mother against the Inspector. ☐

e) Eric returns with Gerald to speak to Mr Birling. ☐

f) Mrs Birling chairs the Charity for Homeless Animals. ☐

g) Mr and Mrs Birling are concerned that Eric has gone out. ☐

THINKING MORE DEEPLY ?

❷ Write **one** or **two sentences** in response to each of these questions:

a) How does Gerald react to parting from Sheila?

....

....

....

....

....

....

b) How is the photograph used in this scene?

....

....

....

....

....

....

c) In what way does the Inspector's authority increase in this scene?

....

....

....

....

....

EXAM PREPARATION: WRITING ABOUT SOCIAL POSITION

Reread the dialogue (pp. 41–2) from **'Inspector:** *You're not telling me the truth.'* to **'Sheila:** *… And can't you see, both of you, you're making it worse?'*

Question: How does J. B. Priestley challenge the Birlings's idea of their own superiority in this scene?

Think about:

- What Mr Birling says
- What the Inspector says
- What Sheila says

❸ Complete this table:

Point/detail	Evidence	Effect or explanation
1: *The Inspector demands the truth from Mrs Birling.*	*Mr Birling demands an apology but the Inspector counters: 'Apologize for what – doing my duty?'*	*The Inspector is not threatened by Mr Birling, the word 'duty' implying that he, at least, will act responsibly.*
2: *The Inspector reminds Mr Birling of his duties.*		
3: *Sheila challenges her parents' haughtiness.*		

❹ Write up **point 1** into a **paragraph** below, in your own words. Remember to include what you infer from the evidence, or the writer's effects.

....
....
....
....

❺ Now, choose **one** of your **other points** and write it out as **another paragraph** here:

....
....
....
....

PROGRESS LOG [tick the correct box]   Needs more work ☐   Getting there ☐   Under control ☐

Act Two, Part 5: Mrs Birling's idea of charity (pp. 42–9)

QUICK TEST ✓

❶ Choose the correct answer to **finish the statement** and tick the box:

a) Mr Birling returns: with Eric ☐   to say that Eric has left ☐
   to say that Gerald has left ☐

b) Mrs Birling claims Eric was: over-excited ☐   sober and sensible ☐   asleep ☐

c) Mrs Birling saw Eva Smith: a year ago ☐   last September ☐   two weeks ago ☐

d) The Committee: refused to help Eva Smith ☐   argued about Eva Smith ☐
   gave Eva Smith money ☐

e) Mrs Birling: did not attend the committee ☐   was chair of the committee ☐
   was an ordinary member of the committee ☐

f) Sheila says that her mother is: an honest woman ☐   dignified ☐   cruel ☐

g) Eva Smith refused to take: stolen money ☐   assistance from the Birlings ☐
   food ☐

THINKING MORE DEEPLY ❓

❷ Write **one** or **two sentences** in response to each of these questions:

a) What is Mrs Birling's attitude to Eva Smith at the committee meeting?

....

....

....

....

b) What is Mr Birling's attitude to his wife's treatment of Eva Smith?

....

....

....

....

....

c) Who does Mrs Birling insist is the main culprit in Eva Smith's death, and what effect does this have?

....

....

....

....

....

EXAM PREPARATION: WRITING ABOUT THE CHAIN OF EVENTS A02

Reread the dialogue (pp. 43–9) from *'Inspector: She appealed to your organization for help?'* to the end of the Act.

Question: What clues does J. B. Priestley give us about where the chain of events will take us?

Think about:

● The women's charity hearing and Mrs Birling's attitude

● What Sheila and the Inspector say

❸ Complete this table:

Point/detail	Evidence	Effect or explanation
1: *Through the Inspector, Priestley reveals a third change of name for Eva Smith.*	*Mrs Birling says, 'First, she called herself Mrs Birling –'.*	*This implies that Eric (the only character left to be questioned) was involved with Eva.*
2: *Priestley discloses the information that Eva was pregnant.*		
3: *Sheila warns her mother not to insist that the father of Eva Smith's child should take responsibility.*		

❹ Write up **point 1** into a **paragraph** below, in your own words. Remember to include what you infer from the evidence, or the writer's effects.

....

....

....

....

❺ Now, choose **one** of your **other points** and write it out as another **paragraph** here:

....

....

....

....

....

PROGRESS LOG [tick the correct box]   Needs more work ☐   Getting there ☐   Under control ☐

Act Three, Part 1: Eric's link in the chain (pp. 50–2)

QUICK TEST ✔

1 Write the correct names by each quotation to show **who is speaking and to whom**:

Mr Birling **Sheila** **Eric** **Mrs Birling** **the Inspector** **Gerald**

a) 'There must be some mistake.' (p. 50)

.... to ....

b) 'You haven't made it any easier for me' (p. 50)

.... to ....

c) 'you're not the type – you don't get drunk –' (p. 50)

.... to ....

d) 'Why, you little sneak!' (p. 50)

.... to ....

e) 'I could have told her months ago' (p. 50)

.... to ....

f) 'Where did you meet her?' (p. 51)

.... to ....

g) 'And I couldn't remember her name' (p. 52)

.... to ....

THINKING MORE DEEPLY ?

2 Write **one** or **two sentences** in response to each of these questions:

a) At the start of the scene Eric says, 'You know, don't you?' What does he mean?

....
....
....
....

b) Mr Birling accuses Sheila of being disloyal. What does this tell you about him?

....
....
....
....

c) When does Mrs Birling's mood change in this scene and what happens?

....
....
....
....

EXAM PREPARATION: WRITING ABOUT ERIC A01

Reread the dialogue (pp. 51–2) from '**Inspector:** … (To Eric) 'When did you first meet this girl?' to '**Eric:** … Oh – my God! – how stupid it all is!'

Question: In this scene, what does Eric's account of his first meeting with Eva Smith tell you about him?

Think about:

- Where he was and what he says about himself
- How he reacts to the Inspector's questions

③ Complete this table:

Point/detail	Evidence	Effect or explanation
1: *Eric had been drinking.*	*'I'd been there [in the Palace Bar] an hour or so with two or three chaps. I was a bit squiffy.'*	*His judgement would be impaired and his behaviour unstable.*
2: *He became increasingly drunk.*		
3: *He had sex with Eva Smith.*		

④ Write up **point 1** into a **paragraph** below, in your own words. Remember to include what you infer from the evidence, or the writer's effects.

....

....

....

....

....

⑤ Now, choose **one** of your **other points** and write it out as another **paragraph** here:

....

....

....

....

....

....

PROGRESS LOG [tick the correct box]   Needs more work ☐   Getting there ☐   Under control ☐

Act Three, Part 2: Almost a father (pp. 52–3)

QUICK TEST ✓

❶ Complete this **gap-fill** paragraph about the scene, with the **correct or suitable information**:

Eric explains that he met Eva Smith again about .... weeks later by accident at the .... He says that they talked, and explains that he was not in love with her. .... is angry because Eric slept with Eva Smith again. The two men quarrel, but the .... intervenes in order to continue questioning .... Eric admits that when he discovered that Eva Smith was pregnant, he was worried about what would happen to him. He says that Eva Smith did not wish to .... him, and that he gave her money, about .... pounds in total.

THINKING MORE DEEPLY ❓

❷ Write **one** or **two sentences** in response to each of these questions:

a) What was Eric's attitude to Eva Smith *after his first meeting with her*?

....

....

....

....

....

b) How can we tell that Eric's attitude to Eva Smith shifted as he got to know her?

....

....

....

....

....

c) How can we tell that Eric is immature?

....

....

....

....

....

EXAM PREPARATION: WRITING ABOUT LANGUAGE **A03**

Reread the dialogue (p. 52) from '*Inspector: But you took her home again?*' to '*Eric: ... – the ones I see some of your respectable friends with –*'.

Question. In this scene, how does the language alter when the female characters have left, and what conclusions do you draw from this?

Think about:

- What each male character present says
- How this compares with any earlier comments

❸ Complete this table:

Point/detail	Evidence	Effect or explanation
1: *Mr Birling uses language more freely in male company.*	'*So you had to go to bed with her?*'	*In 1912 a man like Mr Birling would not refer to sexual matters at all in front of women of his class.*
2: *The Inspector alters his language in male company.*		
3: *We can compare Eric's earlier language with the language he uses in male company.*		

❹ Write up **point 1** into a **paragraph** below, in your own words. Remember to include what you infer from the evidence, or the writer's effects.

....

....

....

....

....

❺ Now, choose **one** of your **other points** and write it out as another **paragraph** here:

....

....

....

....

....

....

PROGRESS LOG [tick the correct box]   Needs more work ☐   Getting there ☐   Under control ☐

Act Three, Part 3: The Inspector's heartfelt words (pp. 53–6)

QUICK TEST

1 Which of these are **TRUE** statements about this scene, and which are **FALSE**? Write 'T' or 'F' in the boxes:

a) Mr Birling is pleased that Eric acknowledges his duty to Eva Smith. ☐

b) Mrs Birling is shocked that Eric stole money. ☐

c) Sheila tells Eric that their mother met Eva Smith. ☐

d) Eric accuses his mother of not trying to understand him. ☐

e) Mr Birling accuses Eric of being hysterical. ☐

f) The Birlings are overcome with grief and fall silent. ☐

g) The Inspector explains that no crime has been committed. ☐

THINKING MORE DEEPLY

2 Write **one** or **two sentences** in response to each of these questions:

a) What is Mr Birling's main concern regarding what Eric has done?

b) How does the Inspector stress the chain of events that caused Eva Smith's suicide?

c) How has the mood changed since the beginning of Act One and why?

EXAM PREPARATION: WRITING ABOUT THE MESSAGE

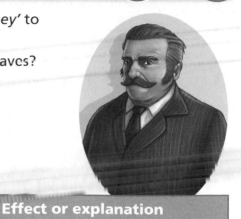

Reread the dialogue (p. 56) from '***Inspector:** You're offering the money*' to '***Inspector:** ... Good night.*'

Question: What is the message of the Inspector's speech before he leaves?

Think about:

- What the Inspector says about Eva Smith
- How he uses the example of Eva Smith to make a wider point

❸ Complete this table:

Point/detail	Evidence	Effect or explanation
1. The Inspector reminds the Birlings that Eva Smith is dead and gone.	'You can't do her any more harm. And you can't do her any good now, either. You can't even say "I'm sorry, Eva Smith."'	It's too late to make amends to Eva Smith for the wrongs done to her.
2: He points out that there are others like Eva Smith.		
3: He warns of trouble for the future.		

❹ Write up **point 1** into a **paragraph** below, in your own words. Remember to include what you infer from the evidence, or the writer's effects.

....
....
....
....

❺ Now, choose **one** of your **other points** and write it out as another **paragraph** here:

....
....
....
....
....

PROGRESS LOG [tick the correct box]   Needs more work ☐   Getting there ☐   Under control ☐

Act Three, Part 4: Raking over the remains (pp. 57–61)

QUICK TEST ✓

❶ Choose the correct answer to **complete the statement** and tick the box:

a) When the Inspector exits Sheila is: crying ☐   laughing hysterically ☐
pacing up and down ☐

b) When the Inspector exits Mr Birling: shouts ☐   collapses ☐
pours himself a drink ☐

c) Mr Birling is afraid he will not: make money ☐   become Mayor ☐
get a knighthood ☐

d) Mrs Birling is ashamed of: Gerald ☐   the Inspector ☐   Eric ☐

e) Mr Birling tells Eric he could: go to court ☐   be called to the Mayor ☐
be sent away ☐

f) Eric agrees with the views of: his father ☐   his mother ☐   his sister ☐

g) The Inspector ☐   Gerald ☐   Eric ☐   returns at the end of the scene.

THINKING MORE DEEPLY ❓

❷ Write **one** or **two sentences** in response to each of these questions:

a) Why does Mr Birling turn on Eric?

....

....

....

....

b) How are we first alerted to the possibility that Inspector Goole may not be an
inspector at all?

....

....

....

....

c) Why does Sheila take no comfort from the possibility that the Inspector is not
a real inspector?

....

....

....

....

EXAM PREPARATION: WRITING ABOUT DIVISIONS IN THE FAMILY

Reread the dialogue (pp. 57–8) from *'**Sheila:** I behaved badly too.'* to *'**Eric:** ... I didn't notice you told him that it's every man for himself.'*

Question: In what way are the younger and older generations divided in their views?

Think about:

- What Mr Birling, Sheila and Eric say
- How Mr Birling and Sheila refer to what has happened in different ways
- What Eric reminds his father of

❸ Complete this table.

Point/detail	Evidence	Effect or explanation
1: Sheila is aware of the important consequences of what has happened.	'But now you're beginning all over again to pretend nothing much happened –'.	She points out to her father that he is still not facing his share of the blame for Eva Smith's death.
2: Mr Birling's opinion of what has happened is different from Sheila's.		
3: Eric sarcastically reminds his father of his view that we should look after ourselves.		

❹ Write up **point 1** into a **paragraph** below, in your own words. Remember to include what you infer from the evidence, or the writer's effects.

....
....
....
....

❺ Now, choose **one** of your **other points** and write it out as another **paragraph** here:

....
....
....
....
....

PROGRESS LOG [tick the correct box]   Needs more work ☐   Getting there ☐   Under control ☐

Act Three, Part 5: Three telephone calls (pp. 61–72)

QUICK TEST ✓

❶ Write the correct names by each quotation to show *who* is speaking and *about whom*. Sometimes it might be more than one person.

Mr Birling   **the Inspector**   **Sheila**   **Eric**   **Mrs Birling**

Gerald   **Eva Smith**   **the Birling Family**

a) 'he behaved in a very peculiar and suspicious manner.' (p. 61) .... about ....

b) 'That man wasn't a police officer.' (p. 62) .... about ....

c) 'I suppose we're all nice people now.' (p. 63) .... about ....

d) 'I was the only one of you who didn't give in to him.' (p. 63) .... about ....

e) 'Just remember your own position, young man.' (p. 64) .... about ....

f) 'How do we know any girl killed herself today?' (p. 69) .... about ....

g) 'you've argued this very cleverly.' (p. 70) .... about ....

THINKING MORE DEEPLY ❓

❷ Write **one** or **two sentences** in response to each of these questions:

a) What are the reasons behind Gerald's return?

....

....

....

....

b) Where does Eric place the theft in the list of his bad behaviour?

....

....

....

....

c) What does Mrs Birling seem to be most concerned about?

....

....

....

....

EXAM PREPARATION: WRITING ABOUT MOOD

Reread the dialogue (pp. 69–72) beginning: *'Gerald: 'Anyway we'll see.'* to the stage directions *'the curtain falls.'*

Question: Discuss the range of moods expressed and why in this scene.

Think about:

- How Mr Birling appears
- How Sheila reacts
- What happens at the very end of the play

Complete this table:

Point/detail	Evidence	Effect or explanation
1: Gerald establishes that there was no recent suicide of any young girls.	'Mr Birling: (triumphantly) There you are! Proof positive: The whole story's just a lot of moonshine.'	The tension lessens. Mr Birling becomes buoyant and jovial at the news.
2: Sheila cannot forget that a girl (or girls) was badly treated, regardless of who she was.		
3: There is a final telephone call to say an inspector is on his way.		

4 Write up **point 1** into a **paragraph** below, in your own words. Remember to include what you infer from the evidence, or the writer's effects.

....

....

....

....

5 Now, choose **one** of your **other points** and write it out as another **paragraph** here:

....

....

....

....

....

....

PROGRESS LOG [tick the correct box]   Needs more work ☐   Getting there ☐   Under control ☐

Practice task

❶ First, **read** this **exam-style** task:

Read the scene (pp. 8–11) in Act One from: '*Birling: Thanks. (Confidentially.) By the way*' to '*Eric: (defiantly) Nothing.*'

Question: What clues in this scene tell you there may be trouble ahead for the Birling family?

❷ Begin by circling the **key words** in the **question** above.

❸ Now, complete this table, noting down **3–4 key points** with **evidence** and the **effect** created:

Point	Evidence/quotation	Meaning or effect

❹ **Draft your response.** Use the space below for your first paragraph(s) and then continue onto a sheet of paper.

Start: *There are several clues in this scene that tell us there may be trouble ahead for the Birling family. Firstly, …*

....

....

....

....

....

....

....

....

....

....

PROGRESS LOG [tick the correct box]   Needs more work ☐   Getting there ☐   Under control ☐

Who's who?

Look at these drawings and **complete** the **name** of each of the characters shown.

Inspector ....

Mr and Mrs ....

.... Birling

.... Birling

.... Croft

....
....

.... , the maid

Eva Smith/Daisy Renton

❶ Look at these statements about Eva Smith/Daisy Renton. For each one, decide whether it is **True [T]**, **False [F]** or whether there is **Not Enough Evidence [NEE]** to decide:

a) Eva Smith came from a country village. [T] [F] [NEE]

b) Eva Smith worked at Mr Birling's factory in the machine shop. [T] [F] [NEE]

c) She was a hard worker and likely to be promoted to a leading operator. [T] [F] [NEE]

d) She also worked at Milton's the hat shop. [T] [F] [NEE]

e) Despite her circumstances Eva Smith had principles. [T] [F] [NEE]

f) If she had had the means, Eva Smith would have wanted to keep her baby. [T] [F] [NEE]

g) She wanted Eric to marry her when she discovered she was pregnant. [T] [F] [NEE]

❷ Complete these statements about Eva Smith:

a) *We never meet the girl who was called Eva Smith or Daisy Renton because …*

....

....

b) *However, we do know that a young girl (or girls) was badly treated by …*

....

....

c) *For example …*

....

....

d) *Gerald also knew the girl …*

....

....

e) *For J. B. Priestley, the girl represents …*

....

....

....

❸ Using your **own judgement**, put a mark along this line to show **J. B. Priestley's overall presentation** of Eva Smith/Daisy Renton:

Not at all sympathetic	A little sympathetic	Quite sympathetic	Very sympathetic
①	②	③	④

PROGRESS LOG [tick the correct box]   Needs more work ☐   Getting there ☐   Under control ☐

The Inspector

1 Each of the character traits below could be applied to the Inspector. Working from memory, add points in the play when you think these are shown, then find at least one quotation to back up each idea:

Quality	Moment/s in play	Quotation
a) Principled		
b) Clever		
c) Inquiring		
d) Mysterious		

2 Look at this quotation from the Inspector. Add further annotations to it by finding suitable adjectives from the bank at the bottom of the page and explaining how J. B. Priestley's words help to convey the Inspector's character.

Inspector: *(taking charge, masterfully)* Stop!

They are suddenly quiet, staring at him.

compelling – shows the Inspector's magnetism

... This girl killed herself – and died a horrible death. But each of you helped to kill her. Remember that. Never forget it. ... You turned her away when she most needed help. You refused her even the pitiable little bit of organized charity you had in your power to grant her. (Act Three, p. 55)

hard-hitting	*polite*	*all-knowing*	*methodical*	*compelling*	*sensitive*
	articulate	*commanding*	*intimidating*	*calm*	

PROGRESS LOG [tick the correct box]   Needs more work ☐   Getting there ☐   Under control ☐

Mr Birling

❶ Look at the bank of **adjectives** describing Mr Birling. Circle the ones you think best **describe** him:

successful	ambitious	caring
popular	awkward	talkative
business-like	self-important	cruel
selfish	dishonest	unjust	middle-aged
shy	hard-headed	gracious

❷ Now add a **page reference** from your copy of the play next to each circle, showing where evidence can be found to **support** the **adjective**.

❸ Complete this **gap-fill** paragraph about Mr Birling, adding the **correct or suitable information**:

Mr Birling regards himself as a man of .... who has achieved a

public position, such as that of Lord .... He is well-to-do, having

made his money from .... , but has little time for those who

.... for him. His most important concern is to achieve a knighthood

and he will do everything he can to prevent a .... from spoiling

his chances. Mr Birling feels no remorse for .... Eva Smith. He is

not affected by the words of the Inspector and when he discovers that the

Inspector may not be what he seems, he even .... about

the events surrounding the possible .... of Eva Smith.

❹ Using your **own judgement**, put a mark along this line to show **J. B. Priestley's overall presentation** of Mr Birling:

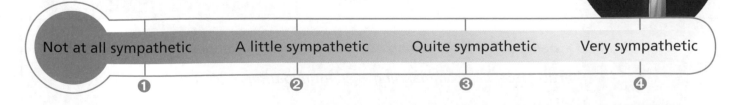

Not at all sympathetic	A little sympathetic	Quite sympathetic	Very sympathetic
❶	❷	❸	❹

PROGRESS LOG [tick the correct box]   Needs more work ☐   Getting there ☐   Under control ☐

Mrs Birling

❶ Each of the character traits below could be applied to Mrs Birling. Working from memory, add points in the play when you think these are shown, then find at least one quotation to back up each idea.

Quality	Moment/s in play	Quotation
a) Cold		
b) Prejudiced		
c) Unashamed		
d) Puritanical		

❷ Look at this quotation from Mrs Birling. Add further annotations to it by finding suitable adjectives from the bank at the bottom of the page and explaining how J. B. Priestley's words help to convey Mrs Birling's character.

forceful – shows she is domineering

Mrs Birling: 'If you think you can bring <u>any pressure to bear upon me,</u> <u>Inspector, you're quite mistaken</u> … The girl asked for assistance … I wasn't satisfied with the girl's claim … and so I used my influence to have it refused … I consider I did my duty. So … I prefer not to discuss it any further' (Act Two, p. 44)

prim	*unsympathetic*	*abrupt*	*unloving*	*forceful*
ignorant	*self-righteous*	*powerful*	*arrogant*	

PROGRESS LOG [tick the correct box]   Needs more work ☐   Getting there ☐   Under control ☐

Sheila Birling

❶ Look at these statements about Sheila. For each one, decide whether it is **True [T]**, **False [F]** or whether there is **Not Enough Evidence [NEE]** to decide:

a) When we first meet Sheila she is described as a woman in her mid-forties.   [T] [F] [NEE]

b) Sheila had never met the young woman before.   [T] [F] [NEE]

c) She had no idea the young woman's name was Eva Smith.   [T] [F] [NEE]

d) She is horrified by the revelation that a young woman has committed suicide.   [T] [F] [NEE]

e) Sheila believes Eric will become a better man as a result of the Inspector's visit.   [T] [F] [NEE]

f) Sheila hopes that her parents will come to understand the Inspector's message.   [T] [F] [NEE]

g) Sheila is determined to marry Gerald come what may.   [T] [F] [NEE]

❷ Complete these statements about Sheila:

a) *Sheila is in a happy mood at the beginning of the play because …*

b) *When she first meets the Inspector she realises that …*

c) *Sheila is greatly affected by the Inspector's news, for example when …*

d) *Of all the characters, Sheila changes the most and she is the one who …*

e) *By the end of the play Sheila's relationship with Gerald …*

PROGRESS LOG [tick the correct box]   Needs more work ☐   Getting there ☐   Under control ☐

Eric Birling

❶ Without checking the book, write down from memory at least **two pieces of information** we are told about Eric in each of these areas:

His background, age and manner	1:
	2:
His behaviour and what he says or others say about him	1:
	2:
His relationships	1:
	2:

❷ Now **check your facts**. Are you right? Look at the following pages:

His background, age and manner: (stage directions, pp. 1–2; Act One, p. 9)

His behaviour and what he says or others say about him: evidence of drinking (Act One, p. 3; Act Three, p. 51); response to Mr Birling (Act One, p. 16)

His relationships: with Mr Birling (Act One, pp. 9–11; Act Three, p. 54); with Mrs Birling (Act Three, pp. 50, 54–5); with Sheila (Act One, p. 5; Act Three, pp. 50, 64–5); with Eva Smith (Act Three, pp. 51–4)

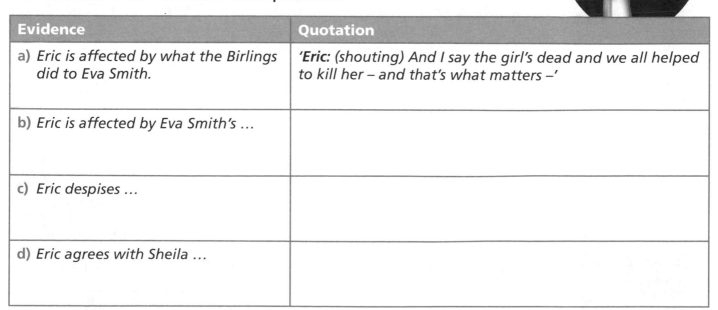

❸ What evidence can you find in Act Three which shows that Eric has been affected by the Inspector's visit? In what way has he been affected? Think about:

● Eric's attitude to Eva Smith and her death

Find **evidence** in the text and include **quotations**.

Evidence	Quotation
a) *Eric is affected by what the Birlings did to Eva Smith.*	*'**Eric:** (shouting) And I say the girl's dead and we all helped to kill her – and that's what matters –'*
b) *Eric is affected by Eva Smith's …*	
c) *Eric despises …*	
d) *Eric agrees with Sheila …*	

PROGRESS LOG [tick the correct box]   Needs more work ☐   Getting there ☐   Under control ☐

Gerald Croft

❶ Look at the bank of **adjectives** describing Gerald Croft. Circle the ones you think best **describe** him:

easy-going	clever	grateful
two-timing	deceitful	unkind
discreet	business-minded	awkward
irresponsible	high-handed	polite
caring	unprofessional	sporty
mature	opportunistic	controlled

❷ Now add the **page reference** from your copy of the play next to each circle, showing where evidence can be found to **support** the **adjective**.

❸ Complete this **gap-fill** paragraph about Gerald Croft, adding the **correct or suitable information**:

Gerald Croft belongs to the upper .... since his parents are Lord and

Lady Croft. At the beginning of the play he is .... to Sheila

Birling. .... considers Gerald to be a good catch not only because

of his social position but also because he has a head for .... ,

like himself. When Sheila discovers Gerald's affair with ....

she is angry, but gives him credit for .... to the relationship.

Gerald was genuinely fond of the young girl and is ....

by her death. By the end of the play he hopes that .... will

take him back.

❹ Using your **own judgement**, put a mark along this line to show
   J. B. Priestley's overall presentation of Gerald Croft:

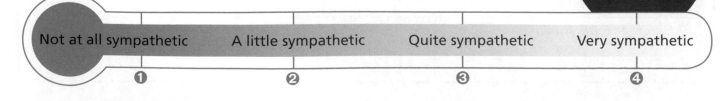

Not at all sympathetic	A little sympathetic	Quite sympathetic	Very sympathetic
❶	❷	❸	❹

PROGRESS LOG [tick the correct box]   Needs more work ☐   Getting there ☐   Under control ☐

Practice task

❶ First, **read** this **exam-style** task:

> Question: Do you think Gerald has changed or not by the end of the play?

❷ Begin by circling the **key words** in the **question** above.

❸ Now, complete this table, noting down 3–4 key points with evidence and the **effect** created:

Point	Evidence/quotation	Meaning or effect

❹ **Draft your response**. Use the space below for your first paragraph(s) and then continue onto a sheet of paper.

Start: *Gerald's role in the play...*

_____

_____

_____

_____

_____

_____

_____

_____

_____

PROGRESS LOG [tick the correct box]   Needs more work ☐   Getting there ☐   Under control ☐

Themes

❶ Complete this **gap-fill** paragraph about the **theme** of **responsibility**, adding the **correct or suitable** information:

J. B. Priestley uses the Inspector as a way of showing how the ....
in society are badly treated. He contrasts the easy, ... life of the
Birlings with workers such as Eva Smith who struggle to survive, particularly
when .... is hard to get.

The Inspector's message about our .... to each other has little
success with either .... or .... However, his
message affects .... , who feels guilt and the need to change his
behaviour. Sheila also accepts her guilt and the wider view that our lives are
all ....

❷ These comments by different characters suggest a particular **theme** in the play. From the list below, choose the best **abstract noun** to identify the theme in each comment.

a) 'Eric: Why shouldn't they try for higher wages? We try for the highest possible prices.' (Act One, p. 16)

....

b) 'Birling: … a police inspector is on his way here – to ask some – questions –' (Act Three, p. 72)

....

c) 'Sheila: It means we've no excuse now for putting on airs and graces…'. (Act Two, p. 41)

....

d) 'Gerald: And I drink to you – and hope I can make you as happy as you deserve to be.', (Act One, p. 5)

....

e) 'Eric: It's what happened to the girl and what we all did to her that matters.' (Act Three, p. 65)

....

equality	history	responsibility
marriage	status	
war	time	humour

THINKING MORE DEEPLY

❸ Complete each statement about the **theme** of **equality**.

a) *When the workers at Birling's company took strike action, Mr Birling was able to dismiss them because ...* ....

....

....

b) *We can tell that Gerald Croft comes from a wealthy upper-class background because ...* ....

....

....

c) *We see clearly the wide difference between Gerald Croft's background and Daisy Renton's since ...* ....

....

....

d) *Sheila's power over Eva Smith's future at Milwards reveals ...* ....

....

....

❹ Write **two** or **three sentences** to show how quotations a) and b) in Question 2 reveal their **themes**. Include a comment on the **writer's effects**.

a) *Eric's comment raises the theme of ...* ....

....

....

....

....

Priestley shows ... .

....

b) *The ending of the play reveals the theme of ...* ....

....

....

....

....

Priestley's effect ... .

....

⑤ Write **one** or **two sentences** in response to each of these questions about the **themes of the play**. Include a comment on the writer's effects.

a) In what way is the Inspector's message in his final monologue linked to the theme of love?

....

....

....

....

b) What does Priestley tell us about Edna's life and what theme is she linked to?

....

....

....

....

c) How did Mrs Birling view her responsibility to Eva Smith?

....

....

....

....

⑥ Write **one** or **two sentences** to show how these comments reveal the character's attitude to the theme of parents or family.

a) '**Birling**: You're just the kind of son-in-law I always wanted. Your father and I have been friendly rivals in business for some time now...' (p. 4)

....

....

....

....

b) '**Gerald**: Hear, hear! And I think my father would agree to that.'

....

....

....

....

c) '**Eric**: But don't forget I'm ashamed of you as well – yes both of you.' (p. 57)

....

....

....

EXAM PREPARATION: WRITING ABOUT LOVE AND MARRIAGE

Reread the beginning of the play (pp. 1–4) from the stage directions *'ARTHUR BIRLING is a heavy-looking, rather portentous man'* to *'Birling: ... for lower costs and higher prices.'*

Question: What do you think Mr Birling's attitude to marriage is and what effect might this have had on his own marriage?

Think about:

- Mr Birling's attitude to Sheila and Gerald's marriage
- What Mrs Birling says

7 Complete this table:

Point/detail	Evidence	Effect or explanation
1: *Mr Birling is pleased that his family and the Crofts will unite in marriage.*	*'we may look forward to the time when Crofts and Birlings ... are working together — for lower costs and higher prices.'*	*His hopes for Sheila's marriage are largely to do with the marriage of the two businesses*
2: *Mrs Birling comes from a higher class than her husband.*		
3: *Mrs Birling acknowledges Mr Birling's commitment to his work.*		

8 Write up **point 1** into a **paragraph** below, in your own words. Remember to include what you infer from the evidence, or the writer's effects.

....

....

....

....

....

9 Now, choose **one** of your **other points** and write it out as **another paragraph** here:

....

....

....

....

....

....

....

PROGRESS LOG [tick the correct box]   Needs more work ☐   Getting there ☐   Under control ☐

Contexts

QUICK TEST ✓

❶ Choose the correct answer about the **context** of the play to **finish the statement** and tick the box:

a) The play is set in the fictional city of: Brough ☐   Brumley ☐   Burminster ☐

b) The stage directions tell us the Birling family are: in debt ☐   landowners ☐ prosperous ☐

c) Eva Smith lived: with her mother ☐   in lodgings ☐   on the streets ☐

d) We learn that the hospital has: an isolation ward ☐   a mortuary ☐ a governing body ☐

e) Milwards: is a thrift shop for the poor ☐   caters for the rich ☐   is a factory shop ☐

f) The play takes place: before the First World War ☐   between the two World Wars ☐ in the 1950s ☐

THINKING MORE DEEPLY ❓

❷ Write **one** or **two sentences** in response to each of these questions:

a) How do we know from the start of the play (Act One, p. 2) that the Birlings see themselves as superior in status?

....

....

....

....

b) In Act Two we learn that Mr Birling's workers were discontented. Why were they unhappy and what happened as a result?

....

....

....

....

c) Why was a customer complaint enough to have Eva Smith sacked from Milwards, despite her being a good worker?

....

....

....

....

PROGRESS LOG [tick the correct box]   Needs more work ☐   Getting there ☐   Under control ☐

| EXAM PREPARATION: WRITING ABOUT HYPOCRISY | |

Reread the dialogue (p. 35) from: '**Gerald:** *She looked young and fresh and charming ...*' to '**Sheila:** *... escaped with a torn blouse–*' and (p. 54) from: '**Mrs B.:** *(shocked) Eric! You stole money?*' to '**Birling:** *... when you found yourself in this mess?*'

Question: What does the dialogue tell you about the kind of hypocrisy that existed in Edwardian society? How do the characters behave?

Think about:

- Alderman Meggarty's and Eric's behaviour
- How the Birlings react

❸ Complete this table.

Point/detail	Evidence	Effect or explanation
1: Mrs Birling is shocked at Alderman Meggarty's behaviour.	'*(staggered) Well, really! Alderman Meggarty! I must say, we <u>are</u> learning something tonight.*'	*Her ignorance of the contrast between Meggarty's public position and private behaviour shows her lack of understanding of the hypocrisy in society.*
2: Sheila is aware of Alderman Meggarty's behaviour.		
3: Mr Birling is shocked that Eric has stolen money.		

❹ Write up **point 1** into a **paragraph** below in your own words. Remember to include what you infer from the evidence, or the writer's effects.

....

....

....

....

❺ Now choose **one** of your **other points** and write it up as **another paragraph** here.

....

....

....

....

....

| PROGRESS LOG [tick the correct box] | Needs more work ☐ | Getting there ☐ | Under control ☐ |

Settings

QUICK TEST ✓

❶ Write the names of characters and events linked to each location. For example, you could write: 'where the body of Eva Smith was taken' by the Hospital/mortuary. Try to include one other example, apart from Eva Smith, of a character who does not appear on stage (unseen character).

The factory

Milwards

Palace Variety Theatre

The Birlings' house

The police station

Hospital/mortuary

THINKING MORE DEEPLY

❷ Write **one** or **two sentences** in response to each of these questions about the **settings** of the play. Include a comment on the **writer's effects**.

a) Where is the play set? Why do you think Priestley wanted a realistic setting?

....

....

....

....

b) How does the lighting contribute to the atmosphere of the setting?

....

....

....

....

c) In what way does the description of Eva Smith's room contrast with the Birling's house?

....

....

....

....

❸ Complete these sentences about the fictional city of Brumley, the conditions of the working people who live there, who controls the city and how.

The fictional city of Brumley is set in ... .

....

....

The working people are employed as ... .

....

....

Their conditions are ... .

....

....

because... ....

....

....

Practice task

❶ First, **read** this **exam-style** task:

> Question: Choose three characters from *An Inspector Calls* and describe their attitude to the theme of responsibility.

❷ Begin by circling the **key words** in the **question** above.

❸ Now, complete this table, noting down **3–4 key points** with **evidence** and the **effect** created:

Point	Evidence/quotation	Meaning or effect

❹ **Draft your response**. Use the space below for your first paragraph(s) and then continue onto a sheet of paper.

Start: *The three characters I wish to focus on all show different attitudes to the theme of responsibility. For example …*

....

....

....

....

....

....

....

....

....

PROGRESS LOG [tick the correct box]   Needs more work ☐   Getting there ☐   Under control ☐

PART FIVE: FORM, STRUCTURE AND LANGUAGE

Form

❶ Choose the correct answer about the form of the play to **finish the statement** and tick the box.

a) The form of a play is its: dramatic style ☐   plot ☐   language ☐

b) A well-made play refers to: a play in three acts ☐   a play with a neat plot ☐   a well-performed play ☐

c) The three unities are: characters, plot, scenes ☐   stage directions, lighting, props ☐   action, time, place ☐

d) The backstory is: the minor characters' stories ☐   events that have happened before the play begins ☐   the playwright's first draft ☐

e) *An Inspector Calls* has been called a whodunit because it is like: a crime drama ☐   a fable ☐   a romantic thriller ☐

f) Eva Smith's story is linked by: cause and effect ☐   Priestley's point of view ☐   the stage directions ☐

THINKING MORE DEEPLY ?

❷ Write **one** or **two sentences** in response to each of these questions.

a) At the end of Act Three, how does *An Inspector Calls* differ from the usual ending of a well-made play?

....

....

....

....

b) Why is *An Inspector Calls* sometimes referred to as a morality play? What themes does it link to?

....

....

....

....

c) What are the main features of the whodunit form that appear in *An Inspector Calls*, and why you think Priestley uses this form?

....

....

....

....

Structure

QUICK TEST

❶ Without checking the play, try to remember in which **Act** each of these scenes takes place:

Scene	Act
1: The Inspector questions Mrs Birling	
2: Mr Birling rings Colonel Roberts	
3: The Inspector arrives	
4: The Inspector's final speech	
5: Gerald leaves the stage after he's been questioned	
4: We learn that Eric has stolen money	

THINKING MORE DEEPLY

❷ Write **one** or **two sentences** in response to each of these questions about the **structure** and **plot**:

a) How does J. B. Priestley build tension at the end of Act One and why?

....

....

....

b) What *two* important twists occur in Act Three?

....

....

....

....

c) How does the Inspector control the action of the play?

....

....

....

....

PROGRESS LOG [tick the correct box]   Needs more work ☐   Getting there ☐   Under control ☐

EXAM PREPARATION: WRITING ABOUT BUILDING TENSION

Reread the dialogue (pp. 47–9) from: '**Mrs B.:** *Secondly, I blame the young man*' to '*Curtain falls quickly.*'

Question: How does Priestley build up tension leading to a climax at the end of Act Two? How does he use the characters to do this?

Think about:

- Mrs Birling's response to the Inspector and vice versa.

- Sheila's response to her mother

③ Complete this table:

Point/detail	Evidence	Effect or explanation
1: *Mrs Birling is insistent that whoever got Eva Smith pregnant should be held to account.*	*'I blame the young man who was the father of the child … some drunken young idler… He should be made an example of.'*	*Builds tension by using Mrs Birling to give clues about the possible father (Eric not yet questioned; fits the picture of 'drunken young idler'.)*
2: *Sheila sees the trap her mother is falling into.*		
3: *The Inspector takes Mrs Birling at her word when she demands that he does his duty.*		

④ Write up **point 1** into a **paragraph** below in your own words. Remember to include what you infer from the evidence, or the writer's effects.

....

....

....

....

....

⑤ Now choose **one** of your **other points** and write it up as **another paragraph** here.

....

....

....

....

....

....

PROGRESS LOG [tick the correct box]   Needs more work ☐   Getting there ☐   Under control ☐

Language

QUICK TEST

❶ First **match** these **words/expressions** to their **meanings** without checking the play:

Word/expression:	Meaning:
a) 'chump'	nonsense
b) 'Steady the Buffs'	office of judge or magistrate
c) 'cable'	fool
d) 'sot'	drinks cabinet
e) 'Bench'	telegram
f) 'moonshine'	drunkard
g) 'tantalus'	keep calm

❷ Now check the **words in context**. Look at the following pages. Do you want to change any of your answers?

a) p. 5 b) p. 5 c) p. 4 d) p. 35 e) p. 10 f) p. 70 g) p. 25

THINKING MORE DEEPLY

❸ For each of the **feelings** listed below, think of a moment in the play when it is expressed. Find a **quotation** to back up each of your examples:

Feeling	Moment in the play	Quotation
1: Sadness	*When Gerald is overcome at the knowledge that Eva Smith/Daisy Renton is dead*	
2: Panic		
3: Happiness		

❹ Now **underline** the **key words** in each quotation that convey the **feeling**.

5 Read these comments from Sheila as she hears the account of Gerald's affair. From the list below choose the best **adjective** to sum up the **tone** of each comment:

a) 'So that's what you think I'm really like. I'm glad I realized' (Act Two, p. 28)

....

b) 'It's no use Gerald. You're wasting time.' (Act Two, p. 33)

....

c) 'the wonderful Fairy Prince. You must have adored it, Gerald.' (Act Two, p. 38)

....

d) 'Go on, Gerald. You went down into the bar, which is a favourite haunt of women of the town.' (Act Two, p. 34)

....

despairing	sad	frank	sarcastic	cold
angry	impatient	serious	bitter	

6 Write a **sentence** to describe how Sheila's **tone of voice** has changed towards Gerald since the start of the play:

....

....

....

In the play several **literary techniques** are used (of which the most important is dramatic irony). Read the **definitions** of these literary techniques:

Dramatic irony – when the audience or a character knows something that the other characters don't

Symbolism – something that represents a big idea or quality (for example, a dove represents peace)

Euphemism – a word or phrase used in place of a harsher one that usually means something unpleasant

7 Complete the table below, identifying the **technique** used in each example/ quotation and giving the **meaning or effect**:

Example or quotation	Literary technique	Meaning/effect
1: *The Inspector*	*Symbolism*	*He is the symbol of conscience, of our need to consider the welfare of others.*
2: 'And one day, I hope, Eric, when you've a daughter of your own' (Act One, p. 4)		
3: 'the girl's condition' (Act Three, p. 53)		

EXAM PREPARATION: WRITING ABOUT THE INSPECTOR'S MESSAGE **A02**

Reread the Inspector's speech (Act Three, p. 56) beginning *'Inspector: But just remember this.'* to *'Good night.'*

Question: What techniques does J. B. Priestley use to accentuate the Inspector's message?

Think about:

- How he delivers his speech
- The effect he has on the other characters

8 Complete this table:

Technique	Example	Effect
1: *Repetition*	*'**We** don't live alone. **We** are members of one body. **We** are responsible for each other.'*	*Stresses key words. The pronoun 'we' emphasises our shared responsibility.*
2: *Long and short sentences in succession*		
3: *Metaphor*		

9 Write up **point 1** into a **paragraph** below, in your own words. Remember to include what you infer from the evidence, or the writer's effects.

....

....

....

....

....

10 Now, choose **one** of your **other points** and write it out as **another paragraph** here:

....

....

....

....

....

....

....

PROGRESS LOG [tick the correct box]　　Needs more work ☐　　Getting there ☐　　Under control ☐

Practice task

❶ First, **read** this **exam-style** task:

Read the stage directions at the beginning of Act One.

Question: How do the stage directions tell us that the play is not set in modern times?

❷ Begin by circling the **key words** in the **question** above.

❸ Now, complete this table, noting down 3-4 key points with evidence and the effect created.

Point	Evidence/quotation	Meaning or effect

❹ **Draft your response.** Use the space below for your first paragraph(s) and then continue onto a sheet of paper.

Start: *In the stage directions, there are several details that tell us the play was not set in modern times. Firstly, …* ....

....

....

....

....

....

....

....

....

PROGRESS LOG [tick the correct box]   Needs more work ☐   Getting there ☐   Under control ☐

Writing skills

1 How well can you express your ideas about *An Inspector Calls*? Look at this grid and tick the level you think you are currently at:

Level	How you respond	What your spelling, punctuation and grammar are like	Tick
Higher	• You analyse the effect of specific words and phrases very closely (i.e. 'zooming in' on them and exploring their meaning). • You select quotations very carefully and you embed them fluently in your sentences. • You are persuasive and convincing in the points you make, often coming up with original ideas.	• You use a wide range of specialist terms (words like 'imagery'), excellent punctuation, accurate spelling, grammar, etc.	
Mid	• You analyse some parts of the text closely, but not all the time. • You support what you say with evidence and quotations, but sometimes your writing could be more fluent to read. • You make relevant comments on the text.	• You use a good range of specialist terms, generally accurate punctuation, spelling, grammar, etc.	
Lower	• You comment on some words and phrases but often you do not develop your ideas. • You sometimes use quotations to back up what you say but they are not always well chosen. • You mention the effect of certain words and phrases but these are not always relevant to the task.	• You do not have a very wide range of specialist terms, but you use reasonably accurate spelling, punctuation and grammar.	

SELECTING AND USING QUOTATIONS

2 Read these two samples from students' responses to a question about Eric. Decide which of the three levels they fit best, i.e. **lower** (L), **mid** (M) or **higher** (H).

Student A: *Eric is rude when Sheila and Gerald are talking. We are told he 'suddenly guffaws'. He cannot say why he laughed and Sheila thinks he is drunk. She says he is 'squiffy'. Both his laughter and drinking makes us think Eric is nervous when he is with other people.*

Level ? ☐ Why? ....

....

Student B: *J. B. Priestley demonstrates Eric's immaturity when he 'suddenly guffaws' at the dinner table while Sheila and Gerald are celebrating their engagement. Eric's inability to explain why he laughed leads Sheila to believe that he is 'squiffy', or slightly drunk, and we can further deduce that Eric is ill at ease in company on important occasions.*

Level ? ☐ Why? ....

....

ZOOMING IN – YOUR TURN!

Here is the first part of another student response. The student has picked a good quotation but hasn't 'zoomed in' on any particular words or phrases:

When the Birlings begin to question whether or not Inspector Goole was a real police Inspector, Eric comments, 'He was our police inspector all right,' which reveals that Eric can be sardonic.

❸ Pick out one of the **words** or **phrases** the student has quoted and write a further sentence to complete the explanation:

The word/phrase '...' suggests that ....

....

....

EXPLAINING IDEAS

You need to be precise about the way J. B. Priestley gets ideas across. This can be done by varying your use of verbs (not just using 'says' or 'means').

❹ Read this paragraph from a **mid-level** response to a question about Eric's relationship with his father. Circle all the **verbs** that are repeated in the student's writing (not in the quotation):

Priestley shows us the depth of Eric's misery when he accuses Mr Birling of not being 'the kind of father a chap could go to when he's in trouble'. It not only says that there is little trust between the two, and shows a father to whom Eric cannot admit weakness, it also says Mr Birling is an unsympathetic man.

❺ Now choose some of the words in the bank below to replace your circled ones:

suggests	implies	tells us	presents	signals	asks
demonstrates	recognise	comprehends	reveals	conveys	

❻ Rewrite your **higher-level** version of the paragraph in full below. Remember to mention the **author by name** to show you understand that he is **making choices** in how he presents characters, themes and events.

....

....

....

....

....

....

....

....

PROGRESS LOG [tick the correct box] Needs more work ☐ Getting there ☐ Under control ☐

Making inferences and interpretations

WRITING ABOUT INFERENCES

You need to be able to show that you can read between the lines and make **inferences**, rather than just explain more explicit 'surface' meanings.

Here is an extract from one student's **very good** response to a question about Mrs Birling and how she is presented:

In Act Two Mrs Birling tries to prevent Sheila from hearing the gory details about Gerald and Eva/Daisy, when she says that it 'would be much better if Sheila didn't listen to this story at all.' This tells us that she still treats Sheila as if she were a child. It also suggests that Mrs Birling thinks that if an unpleasant event isn't discussed, it is as if it didn't actually happen; this is something that seems to separate the older members of the family from the younger ones, who want to get things out in the open.

❶ Look at the response carefully.

- **Underline** the simple point that explains what Mrs Birling is doing.

- **Circle** the sentence that develops the first point.

- **Highlight** the sentence that shows an inference and begins to explore wider interpretations.

INTERPRETING – YOUR TURN!

❷ Read the opening to this student response carefully and then **choose the sentence** from the list that shows **inference** and could lead to **a deeper interpretation**. Remember – interpreting is *not* guesswork!

Gerald believes he is not that much to blame for Daisy's death when he says, 'I don't come into this suicide business.' This shows that he is unaware of the impact he had on her. It also suggests that ...

a) he feels suicidal himself, otherwise why would he refuse to talk about it?

b) by referring to it as 'suicide business' he is trying to distance himself emotionally – he can't face the truth of his involvement.

c) he knows he is innocent so he has nothing to fear.

❸ Now **complete** this paragraph about Sheila, adding your own final sentence which makes inferences or explores wider interpretations:

Sheila is presented as the most sympathetic character by Priestley, and as the one who really understands what happened. At the end, she tells her parents, 'If you want to know, it's you two who are being childish – trying not to face the facts.' This suggests that ... .

....

....

....

....

PROGRESS LOG [tick the correct box]   Needs more work ☐   Getting there ☐   Under control ☐

Writing about context

EXPLAINING CONTEXT

When you write about context you must make sure it is relevant to the task.

Read this comment by a student about Mr Birling:

The situation of the Birling family in society just before the First World War, and the sort of people they are, is partly reflected in the house they live in. The 'general effect is substantial and heavily-comfortable, but not cosy and home-like.' This lack of warmth, but impressive size is particularly like Birling himself, whom we are told later is 'heavy looking' with 'fairly-easy manners.'

❶ Why is this an effective paragraph about context?

   a) Because it explains how horrible Mr Birling is.

   b) Because it makes the link between Birling's home at this time and his character.

   c) Because it tells us what houses were like in the early part of the 20th century.

EXPLAINING – YOUR TURN!

❷ Now read this paragraph and complete it by choosing a suitable point related to context:

The complacency of the Birlings is a key feature throughout the play and mirrors elements of middle-class society at the time. They are unable to believe that anything they did was responsible for Eva/Daisy's situation, and are unprepared for the Inspector's investigations. This complacency can be seen in Birling's words, when he says ...

   a) *'fiddlesticks! The Germans don't want war.' This shows how arrogant and lacking in judgement he is, as we know war was on the horizon.*

   b) *'I think you're a pretty fortunate young man, too, Gerald,' which shows how he sees Sheila as a prize to give away.*

   c) *'it turned out unfortunately, that's all.' which suggests the Eva/Daisy affair was just bad luck.*

❸ Now, write a paragraph about how Priestley uses the context of employment in the 1910s to comment on Eva's treatment by the Birlings in Act One (for example, why she was sacked).

Priestley shows how ... .

....

....

....

....

....

....

....

PROGRESS LOG [tick the correct box]   Needs more work ☐   Getting there ☐   Under control ☐

Structure and linking of paragraphs

Your paragraphs need to demonstrate your points clearly by:

- Using topic sentences
- Focusing on key words from quotations
- Explaining their effect or meaning

❶ Read this model paragraph in which a student explains how J. B. Priestley presents Sheila:

Priestley presents Sheila as someone who develops in maturity as the play progresses. She stands up to her parents telling them that they are both 'being childish – trying not to face the facts.' The use of the word 'childish' shows the extent to which Sheila is now prepared to stand up to her parents.

Look at the response carefully.

- **Underline** the topic sentence that explains the main point about Sheila.
- **Circle** the word that is picked out from the quotation.
- **Highlight** or put a tick next to the part of the last sentence that explains the word.

❷ Now **read** this paragraph by a student who is explaining how J. B. Priestley presents Mr Birling:

We find out about Mr Birling when he says to Gerald, 'I speak as a hard-headed business man who has to take risks'. This tells us that he is a tough businessman and takes chances.

> **Expert viewpoint:** This paragraph is very brief and is unclear. It does not begin with a topic sentence to explain how Priestley presents Mr Birling and doesn't zoom in on any key words that tell us what Mr Birling is like.

Now **rewrite the paragraph**. Start with a **topic sentence**, and pick out a **key word or phrase** to **'zoom in'** on, then follow up with an explanation or interpretation.

J. B. Priestley presents Mr Birling as … ....

....

....

....

....

....

....

....

....

....

....

....

| **PROGRESS LOG** [tick the correct box] | Needs more work ☐ | Getting there ☐ | Under control ☐ |

It is equally important to make your sentences link together and your ideas flow on fluently from one another. You can do this by:

- Using a mixture of short and long sentences as appropriate
- Using words or phrases that help connect or develop ideas

❸ Read this model paragraph by one student writing about Sheila and how she is presented:

Priestley presents Sheila as a young, rather naive woman who seems to grow up over the course of the play. She initially appears immature and lacking in wisdom when she asks whether it was an 'accident' that Daisy/Eva drank disinfectant, implying that she cannot imagine anyone being capable of taking their life in this way. Later, however, she is a changed person. She is able to confront her own behaviour when she realises that she had Eva 'turned out of a job', which is the beginning of her acceptance of her own guilt.

Look at the response carefully.

- **Underline** the topic sentence that introduces the main idea.
- **Underline** the short sentence that signals a change in ideas.
- **Highlight** any words or phrases that link ideas such as 'who', 'when', 'implying', 'which', etc.

❹ **Read** this paragraph by another student also commenting on how Mr Birling is presented:

Priestley gives us a vivid picture of Mr Birling. This can be found in the initial stage directions. He describes him as, 'a heavy-looking, rather portentous man in his middle fifties'. This gives the impression that he is solid and practical. It suggests a no-nonsense kind of person. He is also an older man. The description also tells us he is pompous.

Expert viewpoint: The candidate has understood how the character's nature is revealed in his appearance. However, the paragraph is rather awkwardly written. It needs improving by linking the sentences with suitable phrases and joining words such as. 'where', 'in', 'as well as', 'who', 'suggesting', 'implying'.

Rewrite the **paragraph**, improving the **style**, and also adding a **concluding sentence** summing up Mr Birling's appearance.

Start with the same **topic sentence**, but extend it:

Priestley gives us a vivid picture of Mr Birling … ....

....

....

....

....

....

....

....

....

....

Spelling, punctuation and grammar

Here are a number of key words you might use when writing in the exam:

Content and structure	Characters and style	Linguistic features
Act	character	metaphor
scene	role	personification
quotation	protagonist	juxtaposition
sequence	dramatic	dramatic irony
dialogue	tragedy	repetition
climax	villainous	symbol
development	humorous	monologue
stage directions	sympathetic	euphemism

❶ Circle any you might find difficult to spell, and then use the 'Look, Say, Cover,
Write, Check' method to learn them. This means: **look** at the word; **say** it out loud;
then **cover** it up; **write** it out (without looking at it!); uncover and **check** your
spelling with the correct version.

❷ Create a **mnemonic** for five of your difficult spellings. For example,

tragedy: **t**en **r**eally **a**ngry **g**irls **e**njoyed **d**ancing **y**esterday!   Or …

break the word down: T – RAGE – DY!

a) ....

b) ....

c) ....

d) ....

e) ....

❸ Circle any **incorrect spellings** in this paragraph and then rewrite it correctly:

*At the end of Act Two, the tention builds dramataically as Mrs Birling, 'exchainges a
frightened glance with her husband', and they relise that Eric has been involved with
Eva Smith. By the time the curtain falls, J. B. Priestley insures that the audiense knows
that Eric is the likely father of Eva Smith's unborn child.*

....

....

....

....

....

....

....

❹ **Punctuation** can help make your meaning clear. Here is one response by a student commenting on Priestley's choice of the name 'Goole' for the Inspector. Check for correct use of:

- Apostrophes, full stops, commas and capital letters
- Speech marks for quotations and emphasis

When Priestley gives the Inspector the name of 'Goole', we think of the word 'ghoul' which is another word for 'ghost' or phantom since the Inspector is a mysterious figure and as Gerald discovers, 'in act three wasn't a police officer', the name 'Goole' may well have been Priestleys special choice.

Rewrite it **correctly** here:

....

....

....

....

....

....

❺ It is better to use the **present tense** to describe what is happening in the play.

Look at these two extracts. Which one uses tenses **consistently** and **accurately**?

Student A: *Priestley told us through the powerful character of the Inspector that 'we are responsible for each other', and so emphasised the importance of community. This view is opposite to that of Mr Birling who believed that, 'a man has to look after himself... and his family'.*

Student B: *Priestley tells us through the powerful character of the Inspector that 'we are responsible for each other', and so emphasises the importance of community. This view is opposite to that of Mr Birling who believes that, 'a man has to look after himself... and his family'.*

❻ Now look at this further paragraph. Underline or circle all the verb **tenses** first.

Sheila <u>tried</u> to make her mother understand that she had been building, 'a kind of wall' between the family 'and that girl', Eva Smith. The word 'wall' was an image Priestley used to imply a barrier that Mrs Birling was constructing to protect herself from admitting the truth.

Now rewrite it using the **present tense** consistently:

....

....

....

....

....

....

PROGRESS LOG [tick the correct box]   Needs more work ☐   Getting there ☐   Under control ☐

Tackling exam tasks

DECODING QUESTIONS

It is important to be able to identify key words in exam tasks and then quickly generate some ideas.

❶ Read this task and notice how the key words have been underlined:

Question: _In what ways_ does _Mr Birling_ _respond_ to the _Inspector throughout the play_?

Write about:

- How Birling responds to the Inspector both <u>at the start</u> and <u>as the play progresses</u>
- How Priestley <u>presents Birling</u> by the <u>ways he writes</u>

Now do the same with this task, i.e. underline the key words:

Question: _How does J. B. Priestley tackle ideas about social class and levels of society in the play?_

Write about:

- Ideas about social class and levels of society
- How Priestley presents those ideas

GENERATING IDEAS

❷ Now you need to generate ideas quickly. Use the spider diagram* below and add as many ideas of your own as you can:

*You could do this as a list if you wish.

PLANNING AN ESSAY

Here is the **exam-style** task from the previous page:

Question: *How does J. B. Priestley tackle ideas about social class and levels of society in the play?*

Write about:

- Ideas about social class and levels of society
- How Priestley presents those ideas

❸ Using the ideas you generated, write a simple plan with five key points (the first two have been done for you). Check back to the spider diagram or list you made.

a) *Priestley depicts Mrs Birling's disdainful attitude to servants.*

b) *He depicts Mr Birling's intolerant attitude to his workforce.*

c) ....

....

d) ....

....

e) ....

....

❹ Now list **five quotations**, one for each point (the first two have been provided for you):

a) *'**Birling:** ...Good dinner too, Sybil. Tell cook from me ...'*
   *'**Mrs Birling:** (reproachfully) Arthur, you're not supposed to say such things –'*

b) *'**Birling:**   labour trouble ... . Don't worry. ... We employers at last are coming together to see that our interests ... are properly protected.'*

c) ....

....

d) ....

....

e) ....

....

❺ Now read this task and **write a plan of your own**, including **quotations**, on a separate sheet of paper.

Read from the stage directions *'The INSPECTOR enters and EDNA goes'* (Act One, p. 11) to the stage directions *'and now BIRLING notices him.'* (Act One, p. 13).

Question: *How is the Inspector depicted in this scene and how does Mr Birling respond to him?*

PROGRESS LOG [tick the correct box]   Needs more work ☐   Getting there ☐   Under control ☐

Sample answers

OPENING PARAGRAPHS

Read this task:

Question: *How does J. B. Priestley depict the relationship between workers and employers in the play?*

Now look at these alternative openings to the essay and read the expert viewpoints underneath:

Student A

> *Priestley depicts the relationship between workers and employers in several different ways and circumstances. As the play opens, we see how Edna the Birlings' maid behaves and is treated and the cook is also mentioned. Later we see how Mr Birling treats his workers at the factory, including Eva Smith in particular, as well as the effect Sheila Birling has on her.*

Student B

> *Mr Birling treats his workers badly. They work for him in his factory but he does not want to pay them an increase. So they go on strike. That means Mr Birling sacks the ring leaders without thinking about them. One of these is Eva Smith. So she has to get another job.*

Expert viewpoint 1: This is a clear opening paragraph that outlines some of the relationships to be discussed. It also suggests that these relationships take place in different settings and circumstances. How Sheila affects Eva Smith through Eva's employers, Milwards, should have been mentioned more fully.

Expert viewpoint 2: This opening recounts the relationship between Mr Birling and his workers, without outlining what is to be discussed in the essay, which is the point of the introduction. Other kinds of worker/employer relationships need to be mentioned.

❶ Which comment belongs to which answer? Match the paragraph (A or B) to the expert's feedback (1 or 2).

Student A: .... **Student B:** ....

❷ Now it's your turn. Write the opening paragraph to this task on a separate sheet of paper:

Read from the stage directions *'The INSPECTOR enters and EDNA goes'* (Act One, p. 11) to the stage directions *'and now BIRLING notices him.'* (Act One, p. 13).

Question: *How is the Inspector depicted in this scene and how does Mr Birling respond to him?*

Remember:

- Introduce the topic in general terms, perhaps **explaining** or **'unpicking'** the key **words** or **ideas** in the task (such as 'depict').

- Mention the **different possibilities** or ideas that you are going to address.

- Use the **author's name**.

WRITING ABOUT TECHNIQUES

Here are two paragraphs in response to a different task, where the students have focused on the writer's techniques. The task is:

Read from **'Birling:** *(jovially) But the whole thing's different now'* (p. 70) to the stage directions *'the curtain falls.'* (p. 72).

Question: *What techniques does Priestley use to show the impact of the Inspector's words in this scene?*

Student A

> When Sheila repeats the Inspector's words she says, *'Fire and blood and anguish.'* This tells us that she is afraid about the future if people do not help one another or there is no community spirit. The way Priestley chooses to repeat the words through another character drives home his message to the audience. And as we know there was trouble in the future.

Student B

> Priestley chooses Sheila to repeat the Inspector's powerful words, *'Fire and blood and anguish,'* so conveying her fears for future conflict if we do not care for one another. Not only has the Inspector had a profound effect on Sheila, but also the repetition of these words particularly from the mouth of a member of the wealthy class, reinforces Priestley's message that conflict will certainly occur. Ironically, we know it did, both in the conflict of two World Wars and the General Strike of 1926, when there was wide-scale industrial action.

Expert viewpoint 1: This higher-level response describes the impact that the Inspector's words had on Sheila. It also states the wider implications of the Inspector's words for the audience and gives evidence. It discusses the writer's techniques, using literary terms to good effect. The second sentence is a little long, but nonetheless links ideas very successfully.

Expert viewpoint 2: This mid-level response highlights the effect of the Inspector's words on Sheila. However, the quotation, though appropriate, is not sufficiently embedded in the sentence. There is one instance of the writer's technique mentioned but no others and in the final sentence the point made is not developed and no evidence or examples are given.

❸ Which comment belongs to which answer? Match the paragraph (A or B) to the expert's feedback (1 or 2).

Student A: ....   Student B: ....

❹ Now, take another **aspect** of the scene and on a separate sheet of paper write your own **paragraph**. You could **comment** on one of these aspects:

- Mr Birling's response at the beginning of the scene

- The changes of mood throughout the scene

- The end of the play

Start your plan here and continue it on a separate sheet of paper.

....

....

....

Now read this **lower-level** response to the following task:

Read from the stage directions *'The INSPECTOR enters and EDNA goes'* (Act One, p. 11) to the stage directions *'and now Birling notices him.'* (Act One, p. 13).

Question: *How is the Inspector depicted in this scene and how does Mr Birling respond to him?*

Student response

> When Edna the maid leaves the Inspector stands there, 'he creates at once an impression of massiveness, solidity and purposefulness.' This means he looks big and means business. He also has a habit of staring at people hard so that they get worried. He is not bothered by any of the other characters and they have never met him before.
>
> The Inspector does not want a drink from Mr Birling. He wants to know if Mr Birling knows about Eva Smith and he asks questions. He has a photo that he shows Mr Birling, but he does not show it to the others because he wants to get on and do things his way.

Expert viewpoint: The quotation in the first paragraph is well chosen and gives us a sense of the Inspector's presence, but there is no attempt to embed it in a sentence. Nor is there any exploration in either paragraph of the effect the Inspector has on Mr Birling and how he responds. Comments on what Priestley intends in this scene are needed, and the language the student uses is sometimes too informal, as in, 'means business'.

⑤ **Rewrite** these two **paragraphs** in your own words, improving them by addressing:

- The lack of development of linking of points – no **'zooming in'** on **key words and phrases**
- The lack of **quotations and embedding**
- Unnecessary **repetition**, and poor use of **specialist terms** and **vocabulary**

Paragraph 1:

In this scene, Priestley depicts the Inspector as ....

....

and also ....

....

This implies that ....

....

....

Paragraph 2:

Mr Birling's response to the Inspector is at first ....

....

However ....

....

This links to ....

....

A FULL-LENGTH RESPONSE

❻ Write a full-length response to this exam-style task on a separate sheet of paper.

> **Question:** *How is Eva Smith/Daisy Renton depicted by J. B. Priestley throughout the play?*
>
> Write about:
> - How Priestley presents her through the character of the Inspector
> - How Priestley presents her through the Birling family and Gerald

Remember to do the following:

- Plan **quickly** (no more than 5 minutes) what you intend to write, jotting down **four or five supporting quotations**.
- Refer closely to the **key words** in the question.
- Make sure you comment on **what** the writer does, the **techniques** he uses and the **effect** of those techniques.
- Support your points with **well-chosen quotations** or other evidence.
- Develop your points by **'zooming in'** on particular **words** or **phrases** and explaining their **effect**.
- Be **persuasive** and **convincing** in what you say.
- Carefully check your **spelling, punctuation** and **grammar**.

PROGRESS LOG [tick the correct box]   Needs more work ☐   Getting there ☐   Under control ☐

Further questions (A01) (A02) (A03) (A04)

❶ What do you think J. B. Priestley intended when he created the character of the Inspector?

❷ Which character do you think has changed least by the end of the play and why?

❸ What indications are there that Sheila and Gerald have a future together and from the evidence in the play what would that be like and why?

❹ The structure of the play is carefully worked out. What part does the Inspector play in this?

❺ There are several themes in the play, such as equality and responsibility. What do you think is the most important theme and why? (You can write about a theme not mentioned.)

PROGRESS LOG [tick the correct box]   Needs more work ☐   Getting there ☐   Under control ☐

ANSWERS

NOTE: Answers have been provided for most tasks. Exceptions are 'Practice tasks' and tasks which ask you to write a paragraph or use your own words or judgement.

PART ONE: INTRODUCTION [pp. 6–7]

1 Setting: **The Birlings' House:** All characters (except Eva Smith/Daisy Renton). The entire play is set here. **The Police Station:** The Inspector. **The Factory:** Where Mr Birling runs his business, Eric Birling works and Eva Smith worked. **Milwards:** Where Sheila Birling shops and Eva Smith worked. **Palace Variety Theatre:** Where Gerald Croft and Eric Birling met Eva Smith/Daisy Renton. **Hospital/Mortuary:** Where the body of Eva Smith was taken.

2 Characters: Who's who: Mrs Birling, Inspector Goole, Eva Smith/Daisy Renton, Gerald Croft, Mr Birling, Eric Birling, Sheila Birling

3 J. B. Priestley: Author and context: a) 1906; b) France; c) Cambridge; d) *Diversions*; e) 1926; f) 1929; g) *Journey*; h) talks; i) 1945

PART TWO: PLOT AND ACTION [pp. 8–37]

Act One, Part 1: Celebrating the engagement [pp. 8–9]

1 a) F; b) F; c) T; d) T; e) T; f) F; g) F

2 a) The Birlings are wealthy, prosperous business people. Their daughter is engaged to the son of a lord.

b) Their relationship is affectionate and caring but overshadowed by doubts about Gerald's commitment to Sheila.

c) We learn that Eric drinks too much. He is shy and awkward in company, but can be out-spoken.

3

Point/detail	Evidence	Effect or explanation
1: He believes the powerful and wealthy should protect their position.	'We employers at last are coming together to see our interests … are properly protected.'	His comments imply that he disregards the workforce he employs.
2: He likes to speak at length and expects to be listened to.	He make statements such as: 'Now you three young people, just listen to this – and remember what I'm telling you now.'	He has a high opinion of himself and regards himself as a person of authority.
3: He is confident that future technology will bring prosperity.	He claims that, 'The world's developing so fast that it'll make war impossible.'	He does not take into account other points of view and this clouds his judgement.

Act One, Part 2: A confidential chat [pp. 10–11]

1 a) Lord Mayor; b) knighthood; c) possible scandal; d) clothes; e) claims not to remember something

2 a) Mr Birling understands why Lady Croft might prefer Gerald to marry from within his own class. He uses the possibility of a knighthood to impress Gerald and, through him, Lady Croft.

b) Gerald shares confidences with Mr Birling and compliments him. They share a joke at Eric's expense.

c) Eric is uneasy, and feels excluded from Gerald and his father. He finds it difficult to take a joke.

3

Point/detail	Evidence	Effect or explanation
1: He believes he will be knighted (for contributions to the community).	'I've always been regarded as a sound useful party man.'	His comments suggest that a knighthood will depend on his support for the right people and political party.
2: He believes in self reliance.	He says, 'a man has to mind his own business and look after himself and his own'.	This reveals he feels no responsibility for others in the wider community.
3: He has no respect for the community.	He comments, 'you'd think everybody has to look after everybody else … community and all that nonsense.'	This reveals his hypocrisy. He is happy to receive an honour from the community while believing the community to be worthless.

Act One, Part 3: An inspector interrupts [pp. 12–13]

1 We first meet Inspector **Goole** when Edna, the maid, announces him. Although not a **big/large** man, he is an imposing figure. Mr Birling tries to impress the Inspector by pointing out that he was an alderman and also Lord Mayor and still sits on the **Bench**, meaning he is a magistrate. The Inspector explains that a girl died in the Infirmary after swallowing strong **disinfectant**. A letter and a diary were found in her room. She had more than one name, but her original name was **Eva Smith** and she worked at Mr Birling's **factory/ works**. The Inspector shows Mr Birling a **photograph** of the girl. Eventually Mr Birling remembers that he sacked her because of her part in a **strike** for higher wages.

2 a) Mr Birling wanted to emphasise his importance in the community. He wanted to try to take charge when the Inspector arrived.

b) Gerald agrees with Mr Birling that there was no choice but to sack her. He thinks strictness with the workforce is important.

c) A 'chain of events' is when one event leads to another and each action has a reaction or consequence.

3

Point/detail	Evidence	Effect or explanation
1: Mr Birling cares about the profit his company makes.	'it's my duty to keep labour costs down'.	His comments tell us that he values the profit he makes more than a good wage for his workers.
2: Eric is sympathetic to the hardship Eva Smith faced.	He says: 'He could have kept her [Eva Smith] on instead of throwing her out.'	Eric shows greater concern for people than money.
3: We can further compare Mr Birling and Eric's points of view about taking responsibility for the workers.	'Mr Birling: … if they [his workers] didn't like those rates, they could go and work somewhere else. It's a free country …' 'Eric: It isn't if you can't go and work somewhere else.'	Mr Birling feels no responsibility for what happens to his workers, while Eric does.

Act One, Part 4: Sheila's link in the chain [pp. 14–15]

1 a) the Inspector; b) Eva Smith; c) Eva Smith; d) Sheila, Eric and Gerald know something about Eva Smith; e) factory workers; f) Sheila recognised Eva Smith; g) the Inspector upsetting Sheila

2 a) The Inspector describes in detail the agony of Eva Smith's death. He emphasises how attractive she was and her potential.

b) Mr Birling becomes less assertive and more reasonable in tone. He fears a scandal.

c) The Inspector shows the photograph to one character at a time so that none of the characters know whether or not they have seen the same photograph. This also creates mystery around both Eva Smith and the Inspector.

3

Point/detail	Evidence	Effect or explanation
1: Sheila scolds her father for sacking Eva Smith.	'I think it was a mean thing to do. Perhaps that spoilt everything for her.'	She not only feels sympathy for Eva Smith but also recognises the possible consequences of her father's actions.
2: Sheila begins to realise that Eva is the girl she had sacked from Milwards.	'Sheila: (staring at him, agitated) When was this?'	Sheila asks the Inspector when the sacking took place to confirm her suspicions that she was responsible. She is disturbed by what she is beginning to realise.
3: Sheila recognises the girl in the photograph the Inspector shows her.	The stage directions tell us: 'She looks at it closely, recognizes it with a little cry, gives a half-stifled sob, and then runs out.'	When she realises that the photo is of the shop assistant at Milwards, she realises her part in Eva Smith's downfall and is overcome.

Act One, Part 5: Sheila's confession [pp. 16–17]

1 a) T; b) F; c) T; d) F; e) F; f) T; g) T

2 a) Sheila was jealous of Eva Smith's attractiveness. She also has a bad temper.

b) Sheila reacts with horror and embarrassment at the consequences of her actions. She makes a promise never to treat someone like that again.

c) Sheila's questioning of Gerald about Daisy Renton adds drama to the end of Act One. She also suspects that the Inspector knows more and that there will be more questions to follow.

3

Point/detail	Evidence	Effect or explanation
1: The Inspector deliberately refuses Gerald's request	'Gerald: I'd like to look at that photograph now, Inspector. / Inspector: All in good time.'	The Inspector is calm and increasingly in control of the situation.
2: He states his opinion regardless of whom he is speaking to.	'Gerald: ... we're respectable citizens and not criminals. / Inspector: Sometimes ... I wouldn't know where to draw the line.'	He is judgemental, challenging and authoritative.

| 3: He states the consequences of Eva Smith's dismissal from Milwards. | 'Sheila: ... Did it make much difference to her? / Inspector: Yes, I'm afraid it did. ... she decided she might as well try another kind of life.' | The Inspector is stark and honest about Sheila's part in Eva Smith's downfall. |

Act Two, Part 1: Guilty feelings [pp. 18–19]

1 a) where Act One finished; b) in the doorway; c) laughs hysterically; d) quarrel; e) interrupts Gerald and Sheila; f) unaware of the situation; g) politely; h) does not understand Sheila

2 a) Gerald is afraid that Sheila will find out the details of his affair with Daisy Renton. He is also afraid that their relationship will end.

b) Mrs Birling claims they can't help the Inspector. She tries to make light of the situation.

c) Sheila tries to prevent her mother from being dismissive. She fears her mother's attitude will prove regrettable.

3

Point/detail	Evidence	Effect or explanation
1: Sheila suspects that Gerald is also implicated in Eva Smith/Daisy Renton's death.	She says to the Inspector: 'you haven't finished asking questions – have you? ... Then I'm staying.'	She wants to hear the truth, even if it is unpleasant.
2: But she still feels she is to blame.	'Inspector: And if she [Sheila] leaves us now, and doesn't hear any more, then she'll feel she's entirely to blame'	She could shoulder the guilt entirely, unless she listens to the Inspector's questions.
3: The Inspector discusses shared responsibility.	'Inspector: ... we have to share something. If there's nothing else, we'll have to share our guilt.'	Sheila is affected by his words. She recognises that while she must share the blame she is not entirely responsible for Eva Smith's death.

Act Two, Part 2: Enter Mrs Birling [pp. 20–1]

1 Mrs Birling enters in a **confident/bold/self-assured** manner, which is very different to the mood of the others in the room. When Mrs Birling comments that the Inspector has made an impression on her **daughter/child**, he replies that this often happens with the young. Sheila is determined to stay, despite her mother's comment that Sheila has a morbid curiosity about the girl's **suicide/death**. As the scene develops, Mrs Birling's self-importance increases and she accuses the Inspector of being **impertinent/rude/cheeky**. She reminds him that **Mr Birling** was once Lord Mayor. However, she is shocked to learn of the seriousness of **Eric's** drinking habit.

2 a) The first meaning of 'offence' is 'insult'. The second meaning is 'crime' (you could think about in what sense Eva Smith's death is a crime).

b) The Inspector questions Mrs Birling about Eric's drinking to make her face the seriousness of it. His questioning also suggests to us that his drinking may have a part to play later.

c) Gerald responds honestly, saying that Eric drinks a lot. He also responds sensitively and with regret.

3

Point/detail	Evidence	Effect or explanation
1: Sheila is aware that Mrs Birling does not accept that the family may have played a part in Eva Smith's death	'You mustn't try to build up a kind of wall between us and that girl.'	The 'wall' is a way in which Mrs Birling separates herself (and her family and Gerald) from possible guilt.
2: Sheila is warning her mother what will happen if she fails to answer the Inspector's questions.	'Sheila: ... the Inspector will just break it [the wall] down. And it'll be the worse when he does.'	The Inspector will break down Mrs Birling's defences and reveal her guilt.
3: Mrs Birling fails to understand.	'Sheila: But, Mother, do stop before it's too late.' 'Mrs Birling: If you mean that the Inspector will take offence –'	Mrs Birling is more concerned about good manners than allowing the Inspector to question her.

Act Two, Part 3: Gerald's revelations [pp. 22–3]

1 a) Eric; b) Sheila; c) Daisy Renton/Eva Smith; d) Gerald; e) Alderman Meggarty; f) Daisy Renton/Eva Smith and Gerald; g) Gerald

2 a) Gerald's confession gives us greater knowledge of Daisy Renton/ Eva Smith. His confession also creates greater sympathy for him.

b) Sheila urges the characters not to be evasive; to come to the point. She also suggests the Inspector has foreknowledge.

c) Sheila returns her engagement ring to Gerald. She does, however, leave the way open for a renewal of the relationship.

3

Point/detail	Evidence	Effect or explanation
1: The Inspector asks simple questions.	He asks questions of Gerald such as: 'When did this affair end?'; 'How did she take it?'; 'She had to move out of those rooms?'	These questions, which often build on what the characters say, encourage the characters to reveal further events and actions.
2: Gerald is curious about the Inspector's knowledge.	'Gerald: How do you know that? 'Inspector: She kept a rough sort of diary.' 'Gerald: (gravely) I see.'	The diary is a device that convinces characters (such as Gerald) of the Inspector's knowledge.
3: Gerald reacts to the information about Daisy Renton.	He says, 'I'm rather more – upset – by this business than I probably appear to be – and – well, I'd like to be alone for a while.'	Gerald accepts what the Inspector says and is greatly troubled by his description of Daisy's happy memory of the affair.

Act Two, Part 4: Sheila opposes her mother [pp. 24–5]

1 a) F; b) T; c) T; d) F; e) F; f) F; g) T

2 a) Gerald expected the engagement to end. He does, however, want it to resume at some point.

b) Gerald does not see the photograph. Mrs Birling does see the photograph (but we cannot be sure it is the same one that was shown previously).

c) In this scene the Inspector demands answers. He also makes accusations (for example, of Mrs Birling).

3

Point/detail	Evidence	Effect or explanation
1: The Inspector demands the truth from Mrs Birling.	Mr Birling demands an apology but the Inspector counters: 'Apologize for what – doing my duty?'	The Inspector is not threatened by Mr Birling.
2: The Inspector reminds Mr Birling of his duties.	'Inspector: ... Public men, Mr Birling, have responsibilities as well as privileges.'	The Inspector takes a moral position, suggesting that Mr Birling lacks a sense of duty.
3: Sheila challenges her parents' haughtiness.	'Sheila: It means that we've no excuse for putting on airs Father threw this girl out'	She, unlike her parents, understands that the family have no claim to superiority because of the way they treated Eva Smith.

Act Two, Part 5: Mrs Birling's idea of charity [pp. 26–7]

1 a) to say that Eric has left; b) over-excited; c) two weeks ago; d) refused to help Eva Smith; e) was chair of the committee; f) cruel; g) stolen money

2 a) Mrs Birling is prejudiced towards Eva Smith and feels she is impertinent to use the name 'Birling'. She sees Eva Smith as underserving of help and believes she lied.

b) Mr Birling is worried that the Press will find out about his wife's treatment of Eva Smith. He is concerned about a scandal.

c) Mrs Birling insists that the father of Eva Smith's child is responsible for her death. This creates a dramatic end to the Act, since we learn that Eric is the father.

3

Point/detail	Evidence	Effect or explanation
1: Eva Smith's name changes for a third time.	Mrs Birling says, 'First, she called herself Mrs Birling –'.	This implies that Eric (the only character left to be questioned) was involved with Eva.
2: Eva Smith was pregnant.	The Inspector says, 'It was because she [Eva] was going to have a child'.	The implication is that Eric was the father.
3: Sheila warns her mother not to insist that the father of Eva Smith's child should take responsibility.	She says, 'Mother – stop – stop!' 'Now, Mother – don't you see?'	Sheila guesses where the questions are leading and that Eric is the father.

Act Three, Part 1: Eric's link in the chain [pp. 28–9]

1 a) Mrs Birling to Eric; b) Eric to Mrs Birling; c) Mrs Birling to Eric; d) Eric to Sheila; e) Sheila to Eric; f) The Inspector to Eric; g) Eric to the Inspector

2 a) Eric's words mean that he is the father of Eva Smith's unborn child. He suspects that the other characters know this.

b) This shows that Mr Birling cares more about covering up the truth than finding it out.

c) Mrs Birling's mood changes when she discovers that Eric has taken sexual advantage of Eva Smith. She is then lead away, distressed.

3

Point/detail	Evidence	Effect or explanation
1: Eric had been drinking.	'I'd been there [in the Palace Bar] an hour or so with two or three chaps. I was a bit squiffy.'	His judgement would be impaired and his behaviour unstable.
2: He became increasingly drunk.	He says that at Eva Smith's lodgings, 'I was in that state when a chap easily turns nasty – and I threatened to make a row.'	He became hostile and aggressive.
3: He had sex with Eva Smith.	He says, 'And that's when it happened. And I didn't even remember – that's the hellish thing. Oh – my God!'	He treated her like a prostitute. Later he shows remorse.

Act Three, Part 2: Almost a father [pp. 30–1]

1 Eric explains that he met Eva Smith again about **two** weeks later by accident at the **Palace Bar**. He says that they talked, and explains that he was not in love with her. **Mr Birling** is angry because Eric slept with Eva Smith again. The two men quarrel, but the **Inspector** intervenes in order to continue questioning **Eric**. Eric admits that when he discovered that Eva Smith was pregnant, he was worried about what would happen to him. He says that Eva Smith did not wish to **marry** him, and that he gave her money, about **fifty** pounds in total.

2 a) Eric had little regard for Eva Smith after their first meeting, and could not remember her name. He saw her as a passing fancy and did not arrange to meet again.

b) Eric insisted on giving Eva Smith money when he discovered she was pregnant.

c) Eric claims that Eva treated him as a child, which suggests immaturity. He is more worried about himself than Eva.

3

Point/detail	Evidence	Effect or explanation
1: Mr Birling uses language more freely in male company.	'So you had to go to bed with her?'	In 1912 a man like Mr Birling would not refer to sexual matters at all in front of women of his class.
2: The Inspector alters his language in male company.	He says, 'And you made love again?'	Despite his directness throughout the play, the Inspector also avoids referring to sex in female company.
3: We can compare Eric's earlier language with the language he uses in male company.	Earlier language: 'that's when it happened' In male company: 'fat old tarts'	The first quotation is a vague reference to the sexual act. The second refers to prostitutes, using language that Eric would never use in female company. The change of language suggests double standards.

Act Three, Part 3: The Inspector's heartfelt words [pp. 32–3]

1 a) F; b) T; c) T; d) T; e) T; f) F; g) F

2 a) Mr Birling's main concern is that Eric has committed serious theft. He then starts to plan how to cover up the crime.

b) The Inspector connects the harsh deeds committed to show the characters' shared blame. He addresses each of the Birling family in turn.

c) In Act One the mood is happy and celebratory because of Sheila's engagement to Gerald. In Act Three the mood is one of fear and despair because of the revelations about Eva Smith.

3

Point/detail	Evidence	Effect or explanation
1: The Inspector reminds the Birlings that Eva Smith is dead and gone.	'You can't do her any more harm. And you can't do her any good now, either. You can't even say "I'm sorry, Eva Smith."'	It's too late to make amends to Eva Smith for the wrongs done to her.
2: He points out that there are others like Eva Smith.	'Inspector: ... but there are millions and millions and millions of Eva Smiths and John Smiths still left with us ... all intertwined with our lives'	He is pointing out that we have to be responsible for each other. He is making an appeal for a more caring, fairer society.
3: He warns of trouble for the future.	'Inspector: ... if men will not learn that lesson, then they will be taught it in fire and blood and anguish'	He is saying that without a fairer society there will be social unrest and conflict.

Act Three, Part 4: Raking over the remains [pp. 34–5]

1 a) crying; b) pours himself a drink; c) get a knighthood; d) Eric; e) go to court; f) his sister; g) Gerald

2 a) Mr Birling turns on Eric because he believes he is the one most closely linked to Eva Smith's death. He also thinks Eric's behaviour will affect his own chances of a knighthood.

b) We are first alerted to the possibility that Inspector Goole may not be an inspector when Sheila asks at what point the Inspector arrived and questions whether he is a real inspector. The stage directions also tell us that Sheila is 'sharply attentive' and 'reflective'.

c) Sheila takes no comfort from the possibility that the Inspector is not a real one because, either way, a girl or girls were badly treated by the family. Whether or not Inspector Goole was a real inspector does not change what happened.

3

Point/detail	Evidence	Effect or explanation
1: Sheila is aware of the important consequences of what has happened.	'But now you're beginning all over again to pretend nothing much happened –'.	She points out to her father that he is still not facing his share of the blame for Eva Smith's death.
2: Mr Birling sees what has happened in a different light to Sheila.	He says, 'Nothing much happened! ... there'll be a public scandal ... and who here will suffer from that more than I will?'	Mr Birling sees what has happened only as a threat to his position.
3: Eric sarcastically reminds his father of his view that we should look after ourselves.	He says, 'You told us ... we weren't to take any notice of these cranks who tell us that everybody has to look after everybody else'.	We are being reminded of the Inspector's view, which has affected the younger but not the older generation.

Act Three, Part 5: Three telephone calls [pp. 36–7]

1 a) Mr Birling about the Inspector; b) Gerald about the Inspector; c) Sheila about all the Birling family and Gerald; d) Mrs Birling about the Inspector; e) Mr Birling about Eric; f) Gerald about whether Eva Smith really died; g) Mrs Birling about Gerald

2 a) Gerald returns to bring news that Inspector Goole was not a police officer. He also comes back to make amends with Sheila.

b) Eric considers his mistreatment of Eva Smith to be his worst offence. By comparison, he says, stolen money is not important.

c) Mrs Birling seems to be most concerned that everyone shows good manners. She is particularly concerned that Sheila and Eric behave sensibly.

3

Point/detail	Evidence	Effect or explanation
1: Gerald establishes there was no recent suicide of any young girls.	'Mr Birling: (triumphantly) There you are! Proof positive: The whole story's just a lot of moonshine.'	The tension lessens. Mr Birling becomes buoyant and jovial at the news.
2: Sheila cannot forget that a girl (or girls) was badly treated, regardless of who she was.	'Sheila: ... Everything we said had happened really had happened. If it didn't end tragically, then that's lucky for us. But it might have done.'	She remains troubled and despondent. She has taken to heart the events and the Inspector's message.
3: There is a final telephone call to say an inspector is on his way.	The stage directions read 'He [Mr Birling] puts the telephone down slowly and looks in a panic stricken fashion at the others.'	His jovial mood quickly turns to one of shock.

PART THREE: CHARACTERS [pp. 39–46]

Eva Smith/Daisy Renton [p. 40]

1 a) NEE; b) T; c) T; d) F; e) T; f) NEE; g) F

2 a) We never meet the girl who was called Eva Smith or Daisy Renton because the Inspector holds the information on her (them) and we do not know if this is reliable.

b) However, we do know that a young girl (or girls) was badly treated by the Birling family and Gerald Croft.

c) For example, Mr Birling sacked a young girl from his factory, as one of 'four or five ring-leaders' demanding higher wages.

d) Gerald also knew the girl, called Daisy Renton, and had an affair with her.

e) For J. B. Priestley, the girl represents the workers of the time, the 'millions and millions and millions of Eva Smiths and John Smiths', who were exploited by the wealthy and those with power.

The Inspector [p. 41]

1

Quality	Moment/s in play	Quotation
a) Principled	He wants justice for Eva Smith and those like her.	'Inspector: We don't live alone ... We are responsible for each other.'
b) Clever	He gets the characters to reveal their actions.	'Sheila. ... Well, he inspected us all right.'
c) Inquiring	He feels he must reveal the truth.	'Inspector: It's my duty to ask questions.'
d) Mysterious	There is no record of an Inspector Goole.	'Gerald: There isn't any such inspector.'

2 'They are suddenly ... at him.': compelling – shows the Inspector's magnetism

'This girl killed herself ... forget it.': hard-hitting language – he is tough

'You refused her ...grant her.': articulate – shows he is skilful with words

Mr Birling [p. 42]

1, 2 successful p. 1; ambitious p. 8; talkative p. 7; business-like p. 6; self-important p. 59; cruel p. 71; selfish p. 58; dishonest p. 54; unjust p. 15; middle-aged p. 1; hard-headed p. 6

3 Mr Birling regards himself as a man of **importance** who has achieved a public position, such as that of Lord **Mayor**. He is well-to-do, having made his money from **business/manufacturing** but has little time for those who **work** for him. His most important concern is to achieve a knighthood and he will do everything he can to prevent a **scandal** from spoiling his chances. Mr Birling feels no remorse for **sacking/dismissing** Eva Smith. He is not affected by the words of the Inspector and when he discovers that the Inspector may not be what he seems, he even **jokes** about the events surrounding the possible **death/suicide** of Eva Smith.

Mrs Birling [p. 43]

1

Quality	Moment/s in play	Quotation
a) Cold	Stage directions at start of Act One	'a rather cold woman'
b) Prejudiced	When the Inspector challenges Mrs Birling about Eva Smith's claim	'You admit being prejudiced against her case?'
c) Unashamed	When Mrs Birling states she didn't believe Eva Smith, so didn't regret her actions	'you're quite wrong to suppose I shall regret what I did.'
d) Puritanical	When she discovers Gerald's affair with Daisy Renton/Eva Smith	'I don't think we want any further details of this disgusting affair'

2 'any pressure ... quite mistaken.': forceful – she is domineering

'I used my ... it refused.': powerful – she can control others' lives

'So ... I prefer ... any further': abrupt – she is blunt and direct

ANSWERS

Sheila Birling [p. 44]

1 a) F; b) F; c) T; d) T; e) NEE; f) NEE; g) F

2 a) Sheila is in a happy mood at the beginning of the play because she is 'very pleased with life', having just got engaged to Gerald.

b) When she first meets the Inspector she realises that something is amiss when she hears her father's tone towards the Inspector.

c) Sheila is greatly affected by the Inspector's news, for example when she hears that Eva Smith died, 'so horribly' by drinking disinfectant.

d) Of all the characters, Sheila changes the most and she is the one who recognises the Inspector's message that 'We are responsible for each other'.

e) By the end of the play Sheila's relationship with Gerald has ended, and she is going to consider whether they have a future together.

Eric Birling [p. 45]

1

His background, age and manner	1: middle-class son of Mr and Mrs Birling, early twenties
	2 ill-at-ease, shy, but can also be outspoken, misfit
His behaviour and what he says or others say about him	1: drinks too much
	2: pleasure seeking, immature, looks for the easy option
His relationships	1: poor relationship with his father, who thinks Eric has too easy a life, especially when Eric steals money
	2: uncaring and nasty with Eva Smith at first, but develops a sense of responsibility for her and her unborn child

3

Evidence	Quotation
a) Eric is affected by what the Birlings did to Eva Smith.	'Eric: (shouting) And I say the girl's dead and we all helped to kill her – and that's what matters –'
b) Eric is affected by Eva Smith's courage.	'Eric: ... She came to you [Mrs Birling] to protect me'
c) Eric despises his father's views.	'Eric: ... You told us ... we weren't to take any notice of these cranks ... then one of those cranks walked in – the Inspector.'
d) Eric agrees with Sheila that their parents are ignoring the Inspector's words.	'Sheila: [to Mr Birling] ... You began to learn something. And now you've stopped. ...'
	'Eric: 'And I agree with Sheila.'

Gerald Croft [p. 46]

1, 2 easy-going p. 2; clever p. 62; two-timing p. 34; deceitful p. 33; discreet p. 36; business-minded p. 6; high-handed p. 36; polite p. 2; caring p. 35; mature p. 2; opportunistic p. 34; controlled p. 39

3 Gerald Croft belongs to the upper **class** since his parents are Lord and Lady Croft. At the beginning of the play he is **engaged** to Sheila Birling. **Mr Birling** considers Gerald to be a good catch not only because of his social position but also because he has a head for **business** like himself. When Sheila discovers Gerald's affair with **Daisy Renton** she is angry, but gives him credit for **admitting** to the relationship. Gerald was genuinely fond of the young girl and is **upset** by her death. By the end of the play he hopes that **Sheila** will take him back.

PART FOUR: THEMES, CONTEXTS AND SETTINGS [pp. 48–55]

Themes [pp. 48–51]

1 J. B. Priestley uses the Inspector as a way of showing how the **poor/ workers** in society are badly treated. He contrasts the easy, **affluent/ comfortable** life of the Birlings with workers such as Eva Smith who struggle to survive, particularly when **employment/work** is hard to get.

The Inspector's message about our **responsibility** to each other has little success with either **Mr Birling** or **Mrs Birling**. However, his message affects **Eric**, who feels guilt and the need to change his behaviour. Sheila also accepts her guilt and the wider view that our lives are all **entwined/interdependent/linked**.

2 a) equality b) time c) status d) marriage e) responsibility

3 a) When the workers at the Birling company took strike action, Mr Birling was able to dismiss them because he was in a more powerful position than they were.

b) We can tell that Gerald Croft comes from a wealthy upper-class background because his father is a lord and the family own land and have a large company.

c) We see clearly the wide difference between Gerald Croft's background and Daisy Renton's since the former is wealthy and powerful and the latter is poor and powerless.

d) Sheila's power over Eva Smith's future at Milwards reveals the influence she has as the daughter of a wealthy factory owner.

4 a) Eric's comment raises the theme of 'equality'. He challenges his father, suggesting that their workers have the right to ask for more pay, since Birlings tries to achieve the highest prices for its products. Priestley shows how Eric holds a different set of values from his father.

b) The ending of the play reveals the theme of 'time'. It is a time slip, showing how events are about to repeat themselves with the arrival of a police inspector again. Priestley's effect on the audience, as well as the characters, is one of shock and we wonder how the characters will behave a second time round.

5 a) The Inspector's final monologue calls for us all to take responsibility for each other as part of one society. In this respect Priestley is calling for a kind of universal love.

b) Priestley gives Edna, the Birling's maid, no character development. The effect is that we think of her as one of the millions of poor, invisible people in society who have no power, and she is therefore linked to the theme of equality.

c) Mrs Birling feels no responsibility to help the pregnant Eva Smith. Priestley reveals her lack of sympathy when she refuses help from the Charity, holding the father of Eva Smith's unborn child entirely responsible for her welfare.

6 a) By linking business with Sheila's engagement to Gerald, Priestley shows how Mr Birling views the family as a means of improving his business connections and status.

b) We can infer that Gerald's positive reference to his father means he has a good relationship with him and shares his views, and suggests the importance of the role of the father in a hierarchical society.

c) Priestley shows how Eric is not only ashamed of his parents' behaviour (towards Eva Smith) but also suggests that he is increasingly divided from them.

7

Point/detail	Evidence	Effect or explanation
1: Mr Birling is pleased that his family and the Crofts will unite in marriage.	'we may look forward to the time when Crofts and Birlings … are working together — for lower costs and higher prices.'	His hopes for Sheila's marriage are largely to do with the marriage of the two businesses.
2: Mrs Birling comes from a higher class than her husband.	Stage directions: 'her husband's social superior'	Mr Birling's marriage helped to raise his social standing.
3: Mrs Birling acknowledges Mr Birling's commitment to his work.	'men with important work to do sometimes have to spend nearly all their time and energy on their business.'	Mrs Birling unwittingly suggests that Mr Birling's work matters more than his marriage and family.

Contexts [pp. 52–3]

1 a) Brumley; b) prosperous; c) in lodgings; d) a mortuary; e) caters for the rich; f) before the First World War

2 a) We know that the Birlings see themselves as superior because the parlourmaid, Edna, addresses Mrs Birling as 'Ma'am'. Mrs Birling also reproaches Mr Birling for mentioning the cook in company.

b) Mr Birling's workers wanted better pay. They went on strike and, as a result, the ringleaders, including Eva Smith, were sacked.

c) Milwards would be afraid to offend their wealthy customers. It would be easier to sack a worker than to offend valuable customers.

3

Point/detail	Evidence	Effect or explanation
1: Mrs Birling is shocked at Alderman Meggarty's behaviour.	'(staggered) Well, really! Alderman Meggarty! I must say, we are learning something tonight.'	Her ignorance of the contrast between Meggarty's public position and private behaviour shows her lack of understanding of the hypocrisy in society.
2: Sheila is aware of Alderman Meggarty's behaviour.	'But everyone knows about that horrible old Meggarty.'	Sheila is more aware than her mother of the hypocrisy of people like Alderman Meggarty.
3: Mr Birling is shocked that Eric has stolen money.	'I've got to cover up this as soon as I can. You damned fool – why didn't you come to me when you found yourself in this mess?'	Mr Birling regards himself as an upright and important member of the community, yet is prepared to cover up Eric's theft.

Settings [pp. 54–5]

1 a) The Birling's House: all characters except Eva Smith/Daisy Renton. The entire play is set here.

b) The Police Station: where the Inspector is supposedly based and where Chief Constable Colonel Roberts is linked to.

c) Milwards: where Sheila Birling shops and Eva Smith worked

d) The Factory: where Mr Birling runs his business and Eric Birling works.

e) The Palace Variety Theatre: where Gerald Croft and Eric Birling met Eva Smith/Daisy Renton; where Alderman Meggarty abused Eva Smith.

f) The Hospital Mortuary: where the body of Eva Smith was taken.

2 a) In the Birlings' dining room. Priestley wanted to create a particular effect: a mood that was intense or claustrophobic.

b) The lighting is soft when the play opens. It becomes harsher when the Inspector arrives. Priestley wants to create the effect that the Inspector's inquiries will be harsh and clear-sighted.

c) Eva Smith's room was small and miserable and part of a lodging house. Priestley wants to create a strong contrast with the Birlings' comfortable, wealthy home.

3 The fictional city of Brumley is set in **the North Midlands and is a manufacturing town with a mayor, alderman and police force.** The working people are employed **as factory workers, domestic servants or shop assistants.** Their conditions **in the factories are poor,** because **they are not paid sufficiently well by the wealthy, such as prosperous factory owners, who control the city.**

PART FIVE: FORM, STRUCTURE AND LANGUAGE [pp. 57–62]

Form [p. 57]

1 a) dramatic style b) a play with a neat plot c) action, time, place d) events that have happened before the play begins e) a crime drama f) cause and effect

2 a) Usually, in the well-made play the conflict is resolved and there is a return to normality, but in *An Inspector Calls* there is a twist at the end. The phone call comes as a shock and we realise that events are about to repeat themselves.

b) A morality play is a story with a moral message, rather like a parable, which is a religious story about how you should behave well in life. Priestley's two main themes of equality and responsibility are moral ones.

c) Firstly, when the Inspector arrives he becomes the centre of attention, and we know there will be a serious investigation. Secondly, he questions the other characters very closely as a detective would in a whodunit. Finally, the play unfolds through clues and information. Priestley uses these techniques to create suspense.

Structure [pp. 58–9]

1

Scene	Act
1: The Inspector questions Mrs Birling	Two
2: Mr Birling rings Colonel Roberts	Three
3: The Inspector arrives	One
4: The Inspector's final speech	Three
5: Gerald leaves the stage after he's been questioned	Two
4: We learn that Eric has stolen money	Three

2 a) Tension builds as Sheila realises that Gerald knew Daisy Renton/Eva Smith. The Act ends dramatically, ready for Gerald's revelations in Act Two.

b) Questions are raised about whether or not the Inspector really is a police inspector. There is a second telephone call to say an inspector is arriving.

c) The Inspector decides who will be questioned and when, so controlling what is revealed. He uses the photograph and diary to control the information about Eva Smith.

ANSWERS

3,

Point/detail	Evidence	Effect or explanation
1: Mrs Birling is insistent that whoever got Eva Smith pregnant should be held to account.	'I blame the young man who was the father of the child … some drunken young idler… He should be made an example of.'	Builds tension by using Mrs Birling to give clues about the possible father (Eric not yet questioned; fits the picture of 'drunken young idler'.)
2: Sheila sees the trap her mother is falling into.	'(with sudden alarm) Mother – stop – stop!'	Priestley uses Sheila to build the tension further as we realise that she has guessed that the father is Eric
3: The Inspector takes Mrs Birling at her word when she demands that he does his duty.	'No hushing up, eh? Make an example of the young man, eh? Public confession of responsibility – um?'	The Inspector's words build tension leading up to Mrs Birling's realisation that Eric is indeed the father.

Language [pp. 60–2]

1 a) Chump/fool; b) Steady the Buffs/keep calm; c) cable/telegram; d) sot/drunkard; e) Bench/office of judge or magistrate; f) moonshine/nonsense; g) tantalus/drinks cabinet

3, 4

Feeling	Moment in the play	Quotation
1: Sadness	When Gerald is overcome at the knowledge that Eva Smith/Daisy Renton is dead	'Sorry – I – well, I've suddenly realized – taken it in properly – that's dead'
2: Panic	When Sheila realises the Inspector knows about Gerald's affair and more	'(laughs rather hysterically) Why – you fool – he knows. Of course he knows.'
3: Happiness	When Sheila accepts the engagement ring from Gerald	'Oh – it's wonderful! Look – Mummy – isn't it a beauty?'

5 a) bitter; b) impatient; c) sarcastic; d) frank

6 Sheila's tone of voice towards Gerald has changed from affection at the beginning of the play, to one of sarcasm in Act Two.

7

Example or quotation	Literary technique	Meaning/effect
1: The Inspector	Symbolism	He is the symbol of conscience, of our need to consider the welfare of others.
2: 'And one day, I hope, Eric, when you've a daughter of your own' (Act One, p. 4)	Dramatic irony	Mr Birling (and the audience) are unaware in Act One that Eva Smith was pregnant with Eric's child.
3: 'the girl's condition' (Act Three, p. 53)	Euphemism	The girl (Eva Smith) was pregnant.

8

Technique	Example	Effect
1: Repetition	'**We** don't live alone. **We** are members of one body. **We** are responsible for each other.'	Stresses key words. The pronoun 'we' emphasises our shared responsibility
2: Long and short sentences in succession	Long sentence ending: 'we think and say and do.' Three short sentences follow: 'We don't live alone' etc.	Long sentences show a rapid flow of ideas. Short sentence stresses a key idea. Different sentence lengths can change the tone and can, for example, add tension
3: Metaphor	'in fire and blood and anguish'	Represents 'conflict' or 'war'. Expresses strong feelings

PART SIX: PROGRESS BOOSTER [pp. 64–77]

Writing skills [pp. 64–65]

2 Student A: Level – Mid

Why? The student supports what he/she says with evidence and quotations, makes relevant comments and analyses some parts of the text closely, but the writing could be more fluent.

Student B: Level – Higher

Why? The student analyses the effect of specific words, selects quotations carefully and embeds them fluently in sentences. The writing is persuasive and the points made are convincing.

3 The word 'inspector', as Eric uses it, suggests the Birlings were thoroughly investigated.

4, 5, 6

J. B. Priestley **conveys** the depth of Eric's misery when he accuses Mr Birling of not being 'the kind of father a chap could go to when he's in trouble'. It not only **implies** that there is little trust between the two, and **reveals** a father to whom Eric cannot admit weakness, it also **suggests** Mr Birling is an unsympathetic man.

Making inferences and interpretations [p. 66]

1 In Act Two Mrs Birling tries to prevent Sheila hearing the gory details about Gerald and Eva/Daisy, when she says that it 'would be much better if Sheila didn't listen to this story at all.' This tells us that she still wants to treat Sheila as if she were a child. But, it also suggests that Mrs Birling thinks that if an unpleasant event isn't discussed, it is as if it didn't actually happen; this is something that seems to separate the older members of the family from the younger ones, who want to get things out in the open.

2 b) by referring to it as 'suicide business' he is trying to distance himself emotionally – he can't face the truth of his involvement.

Writing about context [p. 67]

1 a) Because it makes the link between Birling's home at this time and his character.

2 c) 'it turned out unfortunately, that's all.' which suggests the Eva/Daisy affair was just bad luck.

Structure and linking of paragraphs [pp. 68–9]

1 _Priestley presents Sheila as someone who develops in maturity as the play progresses._ She stands up to her parents telling them that they are both 'being childish – trying not to face the facts.' The use of the word (childish) shows the extent to which Sheila is now prepared to stand up to her parents.

3 _Priestley presents Sheila as a young, rather naive woman who seems to grow up over the course of the play._ She initially appears immature and lacking in wisdom when she asks whether it was an 'accident' that Daisy/Eva drank disinfectant, implying that she cannot imagine anyone being capable of taking their life in this way. Later, however, she is a changed person. She is able to confront her own behaviour when she realises that she had Eva 'turned out of a job', which is the beginning of her acceptance of her own guilt.

Spelling, punctuation and grammar [pp. 70–1]

3 At the end of Act Two, the **tension** builds **dramatically** as Mrs Birling, '**exchanges** a frightened glance with her husband', and they **realise** that Eric has been involved with Eva Smith. By the time the curtain falls, J. B. Priestley **ensures** that the **audience** knows that Eric is the likely father of Eva Smith's unborn child.

4 When Priestley gives the Inspector the name of 'Goole', we think of the word 'ghoul', which is another word for 'ghost' or '**phantom**'. Since the Inspector is a mysterious figure and as Gerald discovers in Act Three, '**wasn't a police officer**', the name 'Goole' may well have been Priestley**'s** special choice.

5 Student B

6 Sheila **tries** to make her mother understand that she **is** building, 'a kind of wall' between the family 'and that girl', Eva Smith. The word 'wall' **is** an image Priestley **uses** to imply a barrier that Mrs Birling **is** constructing to protect herself from admitting the truth.

Tackling exam tasks [p. 72]

1 _How_ does _J. B. Priestley tackle ideas_ about _social class and levels_ of _society in the play_?

Write about:

- Ideas about social class and levels of society
- How Priestley presents those ideas

Planning and structure [p 73]

3, 4 c) He depicts how Eva Smith as an employee was at the mercy of Birling and Company if she went on strike for higher wages.

'Birling: ... And this girl, Eva Smith, was one of them [ringleaders]. She'd a lot to say – far too much – so she had to go.'

d) He depicts how socially awkward Gerald sacked Eva Smith regardless of her good record as an employee.

'Inspector: There was nothing wrong with the way she [Eva Smith] was doing her work [at Milwards]. ... All she knew was – that a customer complained about her – and so she had to go.'

e) Priestley shows the double standards Mr Birling uses when Eric, who has a position at Birlings, steals from the company.

'Birling: Gave the firm's receipt and then kept the money, eh? ... You must give me the list of those accounts. I've got to cover this up as soon as I can.'

Sample answers [pp. 74–5]

1 Student A: Expert viewpoint 1; Student B: Expert viewpoint 2

3 Student A: Expert viewpoint 2; Student B: Expert viewpoint 1